Needlework
Patchwork
& Quilting

Jacqueline Farrell

Needlework
Patchwork
& Quilting

HAMLYN

NEEDLEWORK
PATCHWORK & QUILTING

First published in 1999 by Hamlyn
an imprint of Octopus Publishing
Group Ltd
2-4 Heron Quays
London E14 4JB

Publishing Director LAURA BAMFORD

Executive Editor MIKE EVANS
Senior Editor NINA SHARMAN
Managing Editor PATSY NORTH

Art Director KEITH MARTIN
Executive Art Editor MARK WINWOOD
Designer LISA TAI
Production PHILLIP CHAMBERLAIN

Photography DAVID LOFTUS
Photography pages 118–141 DAVID SHERWIN
Illustrations KATE SIMUNEK

The publishers have made every effort to
ensure that all instructions given in this book
are accurate and safe, but they cannot accept
liability for any resulting injury, damage or loss
to either person or property whether direct or
consequential and howsoever arising. The
author and publishers will be grateful for any
information which will assist them in keeping
future editions up to date.

A CIP record for this book is available from
the British Library.

ISBN 0 600 59488 2

Produced by Toppan Printing Co Ltd
Printed and bound in China

Contents

From simple beginnings, patchwork has evolved into a very sophisticated art form over the last ten to fifteen years. This book is designed to appeal to novice and experienced patchworkers alike. The diverse and inspiring projects range from simple rotary cut and pieced items to more elaborate designs incorporating machine embroidery.

Piecing patchwork projects involves a degree of accuracy in measuring and sewing not always required in other creative needlecrafts. However, possibly due to my strong early interest in embroidery, I am a firm believer in getting the feel and balance of a design correct rather than being overly fastidious about construction details such as corners and points meeting.

introduction

Above: *Slashed patchwork throw, page 108.*
Opposite page:
top left – *Masai window covering, page 94;*
top right – *Tribal cushion, page 84;*
below left – *Palazzo tablecloth, page 38;*
below right – *Log cabin sofa throw, page 88.*

Due to their geometric nature, some of the quilts and other projects I see at exhibitions look a little technique-bound. I have tried to redress this in the book by showing the inspiration for each project, drawing from a variety of sources. Indeed, one of the aims of the book is to show the limitless potential of easily sourced images in helping to stimulate your creativity.

Although many of the projects are machine-pieced, there is no reason why you cannot adapt most of them for hand-piecing. It may take a little longer, but your work will certainly be more portable. Quilting by machine is quick and is my preferred method. With today's modern machines, you can achieve many textured effects that will transform the overall look of a finished project.

Try building up your own portfolio of samples inspired by the Techniques section at the end of the book, then tackle some of the larger projects. Stamp your own personality on them by changing the colourways and motifs and hopefully you will create pieces that you can treasure forever.

flowers and gardens

Eternally inspiring, flowers and plants are an easily accessible source of ideas for patchwork and quilting. Regular garden features such as flower beds, paths and hedges can also suggest piecing designs.

Above: *This beautiful detail of a skeletal leaf set against a latticework of grass would inspire crazy patchwork in sheers.*
Opposite page: top left – *The contrasting tones of these strong shapes would make a striking palette for log cabin piecing;*
top right – *The diagonal lines of the leaves meeting at the central stem suggest interpretation into strip piecing;*
below left – *A soft green, yellow and cream colourway is evocative of light, summery table linen;*
below right – *The deep pink folding petals of the rose would translate into cathedral window squares in silks and organdies for a lavish boudoir cushion.*

Despite gardens being full of organic shapes, with a little practice and a fertile imagination you can turn the wildest jungle into a geometric patchwork pattern with the most vivid of palettes. When you are planning a project, try to choose seasonal colours that will match its end use. For example, translucent organzas in a summery palette would be appropriate for light pieced drapes for French windows. A heavier, quilted throw in rich autumnal hues will keep you feeling warm during the colder months. During the summer, collect small flowers and press them in a book for inspiration later on in the year when the garden is bare. Single flower heads provide motifs for quilting lines and flat or three-dimensional appliqué motifs. They can even be dried and added to projects for an unusual touch. Don't forget to take some photographs of gardens in full bloom – these will offer a bright palette to design with during the bleakest months. For simple piecing, a geometric layout is provided by the formal gardens of many stately homes with their borders, mazes and box hedges. If you are interested in garden design, you could look in books for traditional landscape garden plans, which will give you a bird's eye view. Garden structures such as gazebos and greenhouses often have pleasing proportions and isometric designs and may suggest further ideas for piecing.

Right – *This creamy rose is the perfect source for a scaled-down version of log cabin piecing. Make miniature squares in silk for a border on a garment.*
Below – *Softly toothed leaves suggest fabric frills, perhaps with burnt edges, stitched along the sides of a delicate throw.*

Opposite page: top – *Tied bundles of natural grasses look like tassels suitable for decorating curtain tie-backs or cushion corners;*
below left – *Leaves with a simple rounded form could appeal as a design source for curved blocks with a strong colour contrast;*
below right – *This petal pressed onto foil would look wonderful trapped between two layers of sheers, creating a new fabric to stitch with.*

Left – The ridges and veining on the reverse of this leaf suggest quilting worked in different directions, using machine and trapunto techniques.

Right – Layer upon layer of frilly leaves in reddish hues could be represented by chiffon fabric gathered and scrunched to give interesting appliqué textures.

Opposite page – Dark, variegated green leaves, criss-crossing and overlapping, form a spiky, geometric pattern whose linear proportions are appropriate for strip piecing.

Left – Tied bundles of wild flowers could be drawn in a simplified way as a pretty stencil design. Painted onto plain fabric, the motif could then be quilted around the edge.

Left – A lovely natural palette is presented here with soft stone colours and peach tones highlighted with a flash of green.

Right – Quilting using the shadow technique would be a superb method of recreating the subtle beauty of these fallen leaves.

Floral Café Curtain

This pretty curtain has real flower petals and leaves set in translucent organdie panels. It is designed to cover the lower half of a window while still letting the light through. If you do not have a flower press, you can press petals and leaves between layers of kitchen towels under a few heavy books. Dried flowers can be substituted, but they tend to be more brittle.

Materials and Equipment
- 70 x 114cm (27½ x 45in) white cotton organdie
- 100 x 100cm (40 x 40in) natural calico
- White machine sewing thread
- Sewing machine
- Rotary cutter and mat (optional)
- Transparent grid ruler
- Masking tape and pencil
- Selection of pressed flowers and leaves
- Fabric bonding powder
- Iron
- Basic sewing kit (see page 120)

Construction diagram for floral café curtain
(includes 1.5cm [⅝in] seam allowance)

Key

The first dimension given is the width of the panel, the second dimension is the length.

Organdie
A 11 x 85cm (4¼ x 33½in) (*cut 4*)
B 19 x 20cm (7½ x 8in) (*cut 2*)
C 12 x 12cm (4¾ x 4¾in) (*cut 8*)
D 20 x 20cm (8 x 8in) (*cut 2*)
E 20 x 11cm (8 x 4¼in) (*cut 2*)
F 21 x 23cm (8¼ x 9in) (*cut 2*)

Calico
G 24 x 17cm (9½ x 6¾in) (*cut 3*)
H 5.5 x 20cm (2⅛ x 8in) (*cut 2*)
I 24 x 11cm (9½ x 4¼in) (*cut 1*)
J 24 x 14cm (9½ x 5½in) (*cut 1*)
K 24 x 19cm (9½ x 7½in) (*cut 2*)
L 5 x 11cm (2 x 4¼in) (*cut 2*)
M 24 x 27cm (9½ x 10⅝in) (*cut 1*)
N 5 x 20cm (2 x 8in) (*cut 2*)
O 24 x 20cm (9½ x 8in) (*cut 1*)
P 24 x 13cm (9½ x 5⅛in) (*cut 1*)
Q 9 x 12cm (3½ x 4¾in) (*cut 8*)
R 4.5 x 23cm (1¾ x 9in) (*cut 2*)
S 24 x 7cm (9½ x 2¾in) (*cut 1*)

Cutting out

1 Before you begin cutting out the fabric, refer to the diagram and key on this page to see how the curtain is constructed. There are ten floral organdie panels marked A to F. Panel A (leaf) is repeated twice and panel C (daisy) is repeated four times. Each of the panels has a front and a back layer, with the flowers and leaves trapped in between. The curtain illustrated measures approximately 82cm (32¼in) long by 80cm (31½in) wide. If you would like to make a larger curtain to fit your window, add another row or two of decorative panels at each side or at top and bottom.

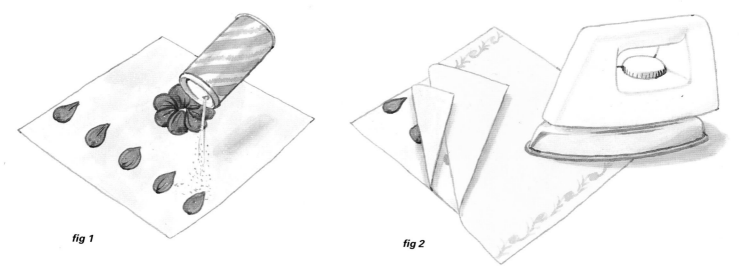

fig 1

fig 2

2 For each of the floral panels, cut two pieces of cotton organdie to the dimensions shown in the key. Using a rotary cutter and mat will make the cutting out process easier (see page 120). On each piece of organdie, stick a square of masking tape marked with the correct letter for the panel. Place all the back layers of the panels onto an ironing board ready for step 3.

3 From your selection of pressed flowers and leaves, make various floral shapes and patterns on the back layers as shown in the photograph on page 14. Use all the petals singly and try not to overlap them too much as this gives dark areas where the light cannot shine through so well.

4 Lightly sprinkle the fabric bonding powder on top of the petals and the background organdie (*fig 1*). Do not sprinkle it heavily in any one area as it will show against the light.

5 Carefully place the top layer of organdie over each decorated panel, making sure the petals do not become dislodged.

6 Lay a pressing cloth or a piece of kitchen towel over each panel and press with a warm iron to melt the fabric bonding powder and fuse the layers together (*fig 2*). It is a good idea to test this process first on scraps of fabric to achieve the correct temperature. The fabric will feel fairly stiff when bonded. Do not use sheets of fusible fabric for this technique, as they make the fabric too crisp and are slightly visible against the light.

7 Again following the dimensions shown in the key, cut out the remaining panels from calico. As before, stick masking tape marked with the appropriate letter onto each piece of fabric.

8 You will now have 37 fabric pieces, 10 in organdie and 27 in calico.In addition, cut 5 strips measuring 30 x 12cm (11¾ x 4¾in) and place them to one side for the tab tops.

Construction

1 Each seam on the curtain is triple stitched so that it looks as neat on the back as on the front. However, only two rows of top stitching approximately 1cm (⅜in) apart are visible on the front of the curtain. Set the sewing machine to straight stitch length 3. Begin with panel B and one of the side panels H. With right sides together and taking a 1.5cm (⅝in) seam allowance, join the long side of H to the long side of B (*fig 3*).

fig 3

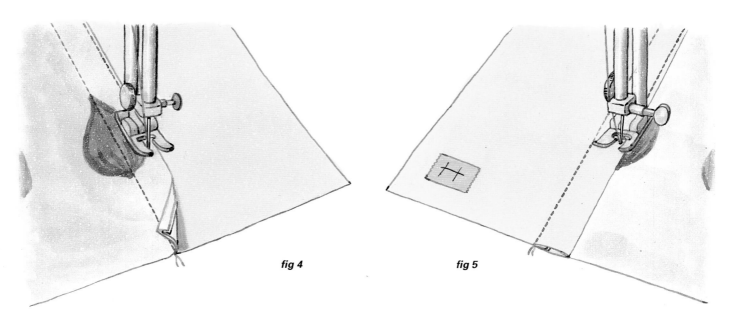

fig 4

fig 5

2 On the wrong side, press the seams together towards the calico and then turn the raw seam edge under by 5mm (³⁄₁₆in) towards the stitching. Press in place. Now stitch close to the edge of this folded seam (*fig 4*).

3 Turn the panels over and top stitch the calico on the right side close to the original seamline (*fig 5*). Repeat this process with the second side panel H.

4 Continue to stitch the narrow calico side strips to the organdie panels in the same way until they are complete.

5 Before you stitch all the fabric panels together to make the curtain, lay them on a flat surface in the arrangement shown in the construction diagram on page 16. This will allow you to check if any pieces are missing or inaccurate.

6 Taking a 1.5cm (⅝in) seam allowance, join the individual panels to make three long decorative strips. Triple stitch each seam as described in steps 9, 10 and 11. The three strips should now be the same length as the two long organdie leaf panels A.

7 Join the three decorative strips to the two panels A in the order shown in the construction diagram, again using the triple stitching method (*fig 6*).

fig 6

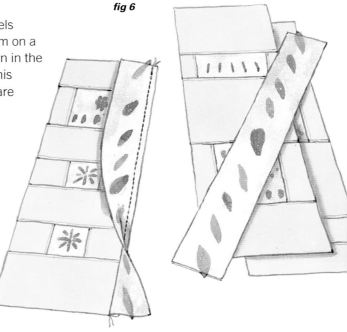

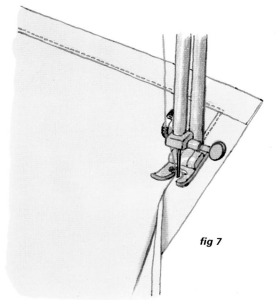

fig 7

8 The curtain is now almost complete apart from finishing the outer edges. Trim these to neaten them if required. Press the raw edges under by 5mm (³⁄₁₆in), then 1cm (³⁄₈in) all round and baste. Stitch around the sides and bottom of the curtain close to the hem edge (*fig 7*), but leave the top edge unstitched. Top stitch around these three sides, close to the outer edge.

Tab Heading

1 To make five tab tops, fold each 30 x 12cm (11¾ x 4¾in) strip in half lengthways with right sides together. Stitch along the long edge, taking a 1cm (³⁄₈in) seam allowance. Work reverse stitching at each end to secure the seam. Turn the tube of fabric right side out and press flat with the seam centred at the back (*fig 8*). Topstitch along both sides twice.

2 Fold the tab tops in half and turn the raw ends up by 1.5cm (⅝in). Pin them on the reverse of the pressed top edge of the curtain, spacing them evenly (*fig 9*). (Add extra tabs if you have chosen to make a wider curtain.) Stitch the top edge of the curtain, catching in the tabs as you go, then top stitch as before. Remove all basting stitches, then trim or knot all thread ends to finish them off securely.

fig 8

fig 9

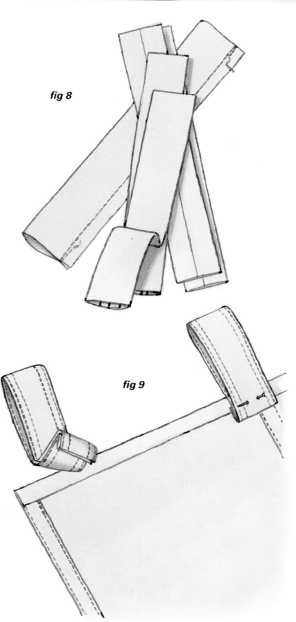

Beaded Hat Band

A delicate summer palette is used for this strip patchwork hat band enhanced with bead decoration. Petals made from shimmering organza are appliquéd to the floral medallions using a three-dimensional technique. The dramatic hand-tied bow adds a final flourish to the band.

Materials and Equipment

- 40 x 25cm (15¾ x 10in) pink dupion silk
- 40 x 25cm (15¾ x 10in) lilac dupion silk
- 30 x 15cm (11¾ x 6in) pale green dupion silk
- 30 x 15cm (11¾ x 6in) cream dupion silk
- 30 x 20cm (11¾ x 8in) dark gold dupion silk
- 25 x 135cm (10 x 53in) pink organza
- 25 x 135cm (10 x 53in) green organza
- 30 x 45cm (11¾ x 17¾in) fusible fabric bond
- 60 frosted pale yellow beads
- Sewing thread to tone with fabrics
- Anchor machine embroidery thread: 1 reel in gold 2724
- Sewing machine
- Ruler
- Fabric marking pencil or tailor's chalk
- Pencil
- Iron
- Basic sewing kit (see page 120)

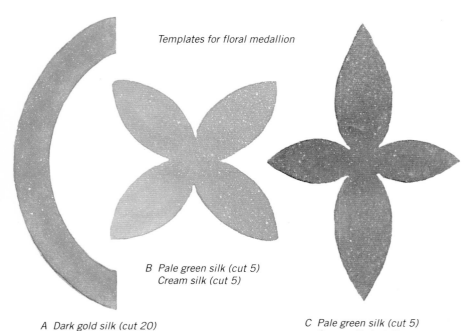

Templates for floral medallion

B Pale green silk (cut 5)
Cream silk (cut 5)

A Dark gold silk (cut 20)

C Pale green silk (cut 5)
Cream silk (cut 5)

Method

1 Using the fabric marking pencil and ruler, mark out five rectangles measuring 8 x 20cm (3 x 8in) on the pink silk. Repeat on the lilac silk. Do not cut out the rectangles until all the appliqué has been completed, as it is easier to work with larger pieces of fabric.

2 Trace the templates for the floral medallion (shown above) onto the paper side of the fusible fabric bond as follows:
template A x 20; template B x 10;
template C x 10.

3 Iron the traced fabric bond onto the reverse of the appropriate silk pieces, following the key given with the templates. Trim around the motifs, then peel off the paper backing.

4 Place a pair of template A pieces centrally on all the pink and lilac rectangles, arranging them in a medallion shape. Iron them in place, then, using the gold machine embroidery thread, edge stitch around them with the sewing machine to secure them.

5 Iron one template B over each medallion shape, using cream silk on the pink rectangles and pale green silk on the lilac rectangles. Repeat with template C, but iron the cream silk over the pale green silk and vice versa. Edge stitch with gold machine embroidery thread as before (*fig 1*).

6 Once all the appliqué is complete, cut out the five lilac and five pink silk rectangles. Alternating the colours and taking a 1cm (⅜in) seam allowance, sew the rectangles together into a length of strip patchwork. Reverse stitch the ends of the seams to secure them, then press the seams open.

7 Fold the length of strip patchwork right sides together and sew the long edges together to form a tube, again taking a 1cm (⅜in) seam allowance. Press the seam and turn the band through to the right side. Press the band, making sure the seam is at the centre back and the appliqué shapes are centred on the front (*fig 2*).

fig 1

fig 2

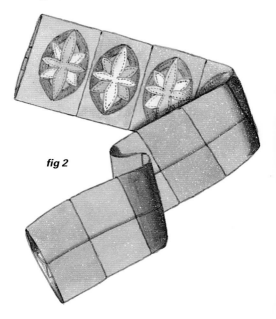

Templates for organza petals

8 Cut the pieces of pink and green organza in half lengthways to create two long strips of each colour. Lay one strip of each colour aside to make the ribbons later. Fold the remaining pink organza strip in half lengthways. Using the petal templates above as a guide, trace 10 large petals and 30 small petals onto the pink organza. Repeat with the green organza.

9 Machine stitch around each petal shape using small stitches (length 2). Trim around the petals, adding a small seam allowance at the sides. Very gently turn each petal right side out and press (*fig 3*).

10 Now take the completed petals and attach them to the centre of each appliqué medallion with a few hand stitches. On the lilac strips, begin with four small green petals to mirror template B. Overlay these with two large pink and two small pink petals to mirror template C (*fig 4*). Sew a cluster of six beads in the centre of each flower to hide the raw petal edges. Repeat on the pink silk strips, reversing the colour order of the petals.

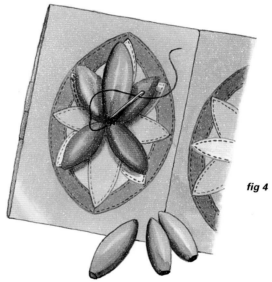

fig 4

11 Take the remaining strips of organza and lay the pink strip on top of the green one. Machine stitch them together all round. Snip the corners close to the stitching. Cut the strip in half to form two ribbons. Turn right side out and press.

12 Fold in the raw ends of the patchwork hat band and press. Slide the raw edges of the ribbon inside the band by about 1.5cm (⅝in) (*fig 5*). Pin and hand sew in place. Use the organza ribbons to tie the band to the hat.

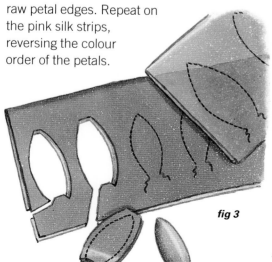

fig 3

fig 5

Autumn Leaf Quilt

In this superb design, the colours of nature are combined with a variety of techniques including stencilling, machine trapunto, shadow quilting and vermicelli quilting. Although the quilt looks very complex, it is not too difficult to construct as some clever tricks have been used to create the intricate effect.

Materials and Equipment

- 120 x 112cm (48 x 44in) printed white cotton
- 120cm x 112cm (48 x 44in) cream organza
- 70 x 112cm (27½ x 44in) peach twinkle organza

- 220 x 112cm (86½ x 44in) white backing fabric
- 40 x 112cm (15¾ x 44in) rust dupion silk
- 40 x 112cm (15¾ x 44in) green dupion silk
- 100 x 112cm (40 x 44in) rust cotton
- 130 x 150cm (51 x 59in) 170g (6oz) wadding
- 160 x 150cm (63 x 59in) 57g (2oz) wadding
- 120 x 112cm (48 x 44in) light-weight iron-on interfacing
- Anchor machine embroidery threads: one reel in each of cream 2107 and peach 2308
- Invisible nylon machine thread
- Sewing thread in ivory and rust
- Sewing machine
- Rotary cutter and mat
- Transparent grid ruler
- Craft knife
- 30 x 40cm (12 x 15¾in) stencil card
- Small stencil brush
- Selection of acrylic paints in autumnal shades, or red, yellow and blue to mix
- Paint palette or old plate
- Dressmakers' carbon paper
- Quilters' safety pins
- Masking tape 2.5cm (1in) wide
- Iron
- Basic sewing kit (see page 120)

Template for leaf sprig (shown actual size)

Stencilling

1 Trace the template for the leaf sprig shown here onto stencil card and cut out the shapes with a craft knife. Using the acrylic paints, mix random autumnal colours plus a few greens on a palette or old plate.

2 From the printed white cotton, cut a square measuring 66 x 66cm (26 x 26in). Fold it in half diagonally each way and press lightly to mark a cross. Each arm of the cross will have a sprig of leaves stencilled over it. Secure the fabric to a flat surface with masking tape, tape the cut stencil on top and dab the paint onto the fabric with the dry stencil brush. Work inwards from the cut edges, blending the colours as you go (*fig 1*). Clean the brush by rubbing it on sheets of paper towel. Stencil all four leaf sprigs. You can elaborate on the basic design by adding extra leaves if you wish. Fix with a cool iron, placing an old pressing cloth over the motifs to keep the iron clean.

fig 1

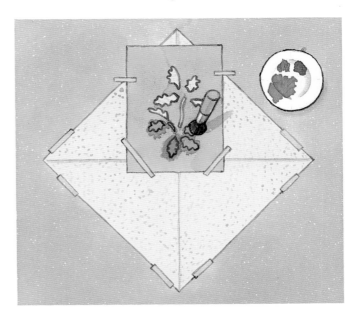

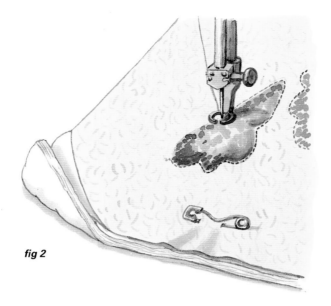

fig 2

fig 3

Construction

1 Cut a piece of the 170g (6oz) wadding measuring 66 x 66cm (26 x 26in) and pin to the back of the stencilled cotton square using quilters' safety pins. Set up the sewing machine for free embroidery (see page 134). Using invisible thread, stitch around the outer edges of the leaves (*fig 2*). Trim away the excess wadding from around each leaf.

2 Prepare the corner patches for the borders next. Cut eight 12cm (4¾in) squares from the printed white cotton and stencil a single leaf onto each one, as in step 2. Stitch 170g (6oz) wadding to the back, quilt and trim as above. Cut out eight squares of cream organza and pin one on top of each corner patch (*fig 3*).

3 Now make the border strips. From the iron-on interfacing, cut four strips 12 x 66cm (4¾ x 26in) for the inner border and eight strips 12cm x 54cm (4¾ x 21¼in) for the outer border.

4 Lay the strips on an ironing board, glue side up. Snip scraps of rust and green silk and printed white cotton over them at random until the interfacing is covered. Using a pressing cloth to protect the iron, iron the scraps in place (*fig 4*). Cut strips of cream organza the same size as the borders, lay them over the top and pin in place.

fig 4

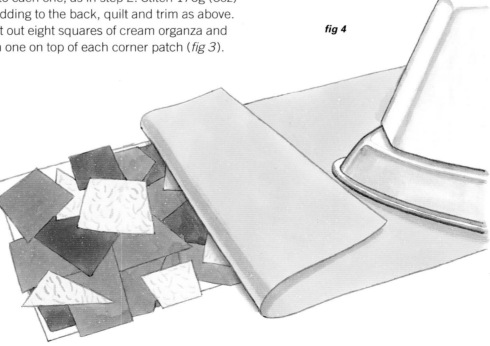

5 With right sides together, join two of the inner borders to opposite sides of the quilt centre, using ivory thread and taking a 1.5cm (⅝in) seam allowance. Stitch corners to each end of the two remaining inner borders and join to the remaining two sides of the quilt centre (*fig 5*).

6 Trace the template for the leaf border shown below and transfer onto the organza borders with dressmakers' carbon paper (see page 121). Repeat as many times as required. You can also add further stencilled single leaves at this stage, overlapping them from the quilt centre onto the border. Refer to the main photograph for suggestions.

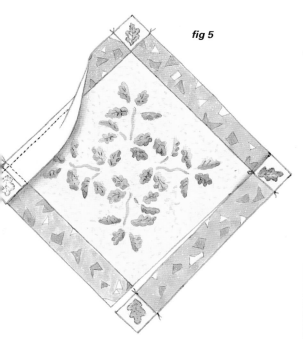

fig 5

Template for leaf border

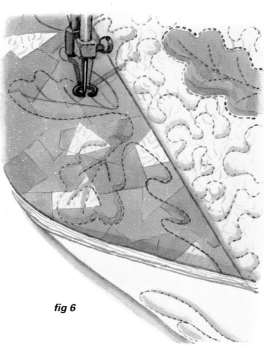

fig 6

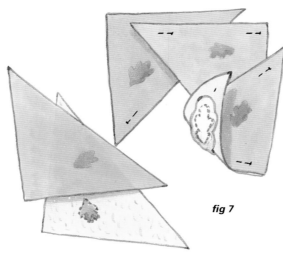

fig 7

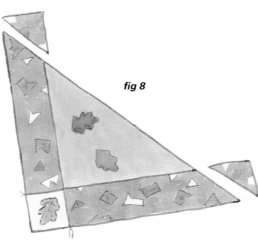

fig 8

7 Lay the quilt centre and inner border onto a piece of 57g (2oz) wadding and a piece of backing fabric cut to the same size. Pin through all layers. Set up the sewing machine for free embroidery. Using cream thread, quilt around the leaves and stems, adding veins to the leaves. Work vermicelli stitch (see page 135) around the white background in order to flatten the wadding and allow the leaves to stand proud. Change to the peach thread and stitch the border pattern (*fig 6*) to create shadow quilting (see page 133).

8 To make the triangular corners, cut four large right-angled triangles from the printed white cotton measuring 46cm (18in) on two sides and 63cm (24in) on the third side. Stencil leaves on them at random, then quilt and trim as in step 3. Cut four pieces of peach organza to fit the triangles. Lay them over the triangles and pin in place (*fig 7*).

9 Take one of the strips prepared for the outer border (see steps 5 and 6) and join it to a short side of one of the triangles, taking a 1.5cm (⅝in) seam allowance. Stitch a corner patch to a second border strip and join to the other short side of the triangle. Cut one end of each border at a 45° angle to line up with the diagonal edge of the triangle (*fig 8*). Repeat with the other three triangles.

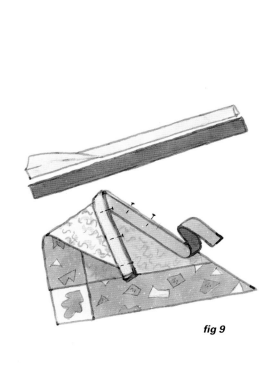

fig 9

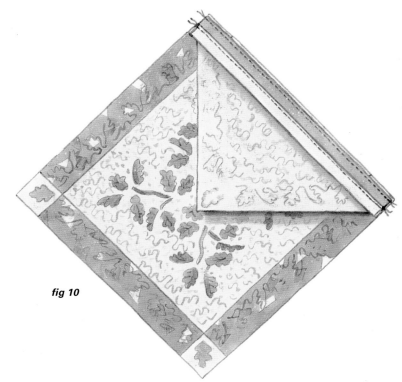

fig 10

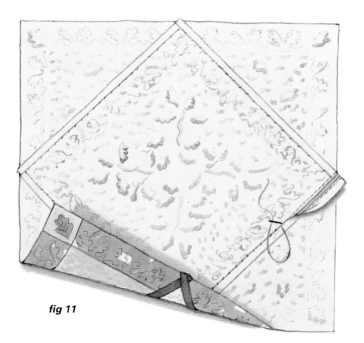

fig 11

10 Lay the triangles onto 57g (2oz) wadding and the backing fabric, cut to size. Using the peach thread, quilt around the leaves and cover the background with vermicelli stitch as in step 9. Shadow quilt the borders as before. Trim 1cm (⅜in) off the long edge of the triangle and around the inner quilt borders.

Sashings

1 Use the rust cotton for the sashings. Cut four strips 2.5cm (1in) wide x the long side of each triangle. Cut four strips 4.5cm (1¾in) wide x the long side of each triangle. Fold the 4.5cm (1¾in) wide strips in half and press. Pin a folded strip onto the wrong side of each triangle, matching the raw edges. Pin a 2.5cm (1in) strip right sides together on top of each triangle (*fig 9*). Sew through all layers, using rust thread and taking a 5mm (¾₆in) seam.

2 Open out the single piece of sashing on each triangle. Lay each triangle onto the quilt centre, right sides together and matching the raw edge of the single sashing to the raw edge of the quilt. Stitch, taking a 5mm (¾₆in) seam allowance (*fig 10*). Open out and finger press. On the wrong side of the quilt, fold over the folded strip to cover the join and slip stitch in place (*fig 11*).

3 To make the final border strips, measure the finished sides of the quilt and cut strips 3.5cm (1⅜in) wide from the rust cotton to fit, joining them to make up the length. Add 1.5cm (⅝in) turnings at each end of two of them. Pin the two shorter strips to opposite sides of the quilt, right sides together. Stitch, taking a 5mm (¾₆in) seam allowance. Turn to the back, fold the raw edges under and slip stitch in place. Repeat for the remaining two sides, tucking under the turnings at each end.

city and architecture

Above: *Tile patterns with flowing lines make ideal quilting motifs. This design could be repeated to fit a square cushion.*
Opposite page: top left – *Hexagonal floor tiles simply require a straightforward translation into English patchwork. You could dye your fabric in brick shades first;*
top right – *The opulent colours of stained glass provide one of the most dramatic palettes for any patchwork project;*
below left – *For a stained glass look, apply fabric to a background and cover the joins with black bias binding to imitate leading;*
below right – *This stone archway could be simplified into a curved patchwork block with radiating lines of quilting. Keep to neutral shades for a subtle effect.*

City architecture is one of the best and most obvious design sources for patchwork. All around us, buildings are constructed on geometric principles enhanced with interesting details.

Architectural features in all their variety provide a wealth of ideas for patchwork projects, as do interiors of buildings. The projects in this section, for example, take roof and floor tiles and a stained glass window as inspiration. In Glasgow in Scotland, where I studied art, Victorian Gothic-style churches abound. These suggest detailed quilted lines over intricate pieced backgrounds. By contrast, Art Deco architecture offers curves and flowing lines that can be more simply pieced and quilted, or alluded to with colour-washed fabric patches. Travel books offer a visual feast of architecture from Gaudi's decadent towers in Barcelona in Spain to tall, elegant Parisian town houses with their repetitive pattern of ornate windows and wrought-iron balconies. Building sites, too, are an excellent source of reference with steel girders, scaffolding and ladders providing a grid of rectangles, squares and triangles that would piece together in an unusual way and give depth to a project. You could take photographs of building sites, then cut 3 x 3cm (1¼ x 1¼in) window mounts and place them over different parts of your photos to isolate potential areas to use in designing a patchwork block. Alternatively, you could cut up your photos and weave them back together to create an all-over design for strip piecing. Viewed creatively, the buildings around you have endless potential as design sources.

Right – *Carved stone windows show shape and depth reminiscent of the cathedral window technique. Extra detail can be added with rouleau tubes, rolled and twisted before being applied on top.*
Below – *This carved cross could be squared off and block pieced for a bold repeating design.*

Opposite page: top – *Enlarge a photograph like this one, then simply trace around each brick, add seam allowances and you have an instant design for piecing;*
below left – *The linear shapes of this wrought iron fence would look beautiful quilted as a border design or a centre medallion;*
below right – *Bricks naturally suggest pieced rectangles, but consider using trapunto quilting for a cushion or pillow in order to add more texture and light and shade.*

Left – This fragmented stained glass design already looks rather like crazy patchwork. Imitate the glowing colours with satins and velvets.

Right – Stark lines are created where these ornamental chimney pots and rooftops meet the sky. Use the shapes as a suggestion for an unusual edge along a throw.

Opposite page – This image of an ornate carving set into a concave brick wall only needs to be mirrored before being made into a quilting design.

Left – Bold, distinctive motifs such as the ones on this crest translate most effectively into appliqué. Make the images more interesting by padding and quilting them, adding the features with hand or machine embroidery.

Left – These tiles give a terracotta palette from palest peach to brick red. The lines of cement provide a lighter contrast colour suitable for a quilting thread.

Right – Crumbling brick overgrown with moss suggests lavish machine quilting with shadow quilted details. Combine with a decorative edge like the one suggested by the chimney stacks above.

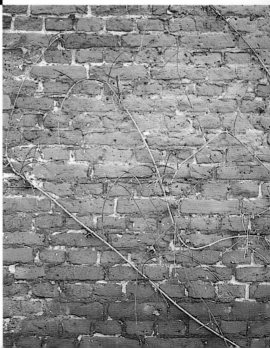

Palazzo Tablecloth

Many stately buildings have magnificent features with intricate design details. In particular, the regular geometric patterns found in tiled floors are often ideal to interpret in patchwork. In order to emphasize the architectural theme, the colours for this tablecloth were deliberately chosen in neutral stone shades, although the project would look equally impressive worked in a stronger range of colours.

Materials and Equipment

- 1m (1⅛yd) craft cotton 112cm (44in) wide in each of textured white (striped) and textured cream (checked)
- 2m (2⅛yd) craft cotton 112cm (44in) wide in textured beige (striped)
- 1.10m (1¼yd) craft cotton 112cm (44in) wide in textured stone (marbled)
- 130 x 130cm (51 x 51in) cream backing fabric
- 20 x 30cm (8 x 11¾in) woven gold lamé
- 20 x 30cm (8 x 11¾in) fusible fabric bond
- White sewing thread
- Anchor machine embroidery thread: one reel in Cristalle metallic gold
- Sewing machine
- Rotary cutter and mat
- Transparent grid ruler
- Template plastic or card
- Tracing paper
- Pencil
- Quilters' safety pins
- Iron
- Basic sewing kit (see page 120)

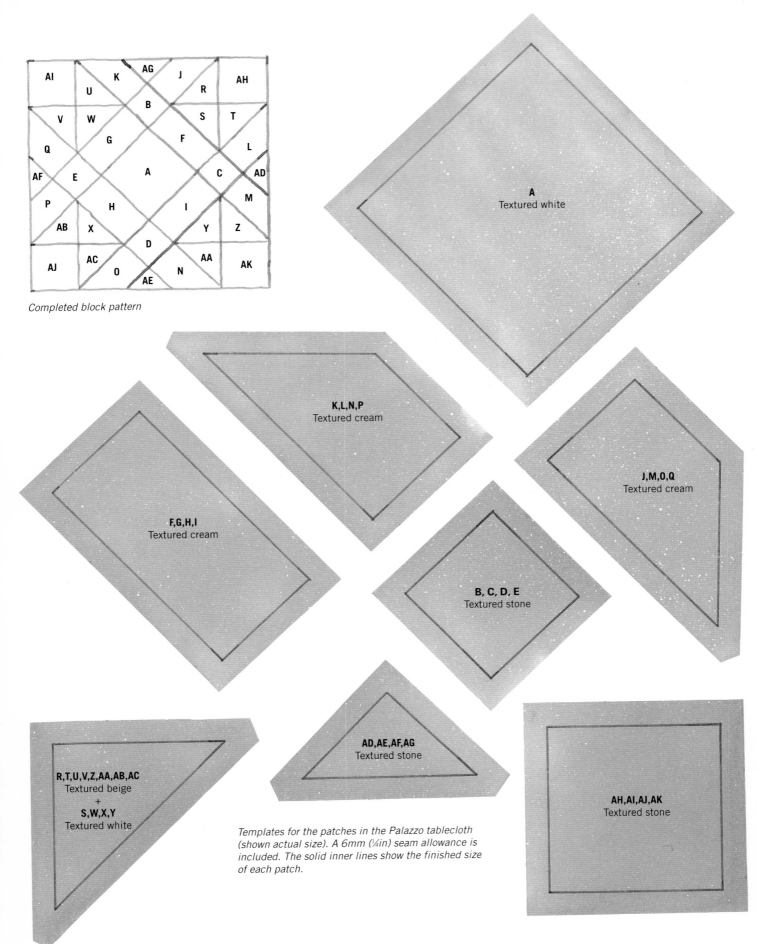

Completed block pattern

A
Textured white

K,L,N,P
Textured cream

J,M,O,Q
Textured cream

F,G,H,I
Textured cream

B, C, D, E
Textured stone

R,T,U,V,Z,AA,AB,AC
Textured beige
+
S,W,X,Y
Textured white

AD,AE,AF,AG
Textured stone

AH,AI,AJ,AK
Textured stone

Templates for the patches in the Palazzo tablecloth (shown actual size). A 6mm (¼in) seam allowance is included. The solid inner lines show the finished size of each patch.

Method

1 Each block in this project is made up of 37 patches of fabric. There are 25 blocks, so a total of 925 patches need to be cut for the tablecloth. Templates have been given for the main shapes that repeat within the block (see opposite). Trace all 37 patch shapes for one block onto paper, mark with the appropriate letter and colourway and cut out for reference.

2 Make a template for each type of patch from plastic or card (see page 122). Mark each one 25 times onto the correct fabric. With striped fabric, check that the stripes go in the right direction each time. Cut out the patches using scissors or a rotary cutter and mat. As you cut them, place them in piles and pin the correct paper shape on top of each pile for easy reference. Lay the piles on a flat surface in the block pattern (opposite top) to check that the patches are cut correctly.

3 This project has been machine-pieced, but you could hand-piece it if you prefer. All seam allowances are 6mm (¼in). If you are joining the patches by hand, mark the seam allowance on the wrong side of the fabric with a quilters' quarter and quilt marker. There is no need to mark the fabric if you are machine-piecing (*fig 1*).

4 Set your sewing machine to stitch length 3. Using white sewing thread, stitch the patches together section by section in the following piecing order (*fig 2*). (Letters in brackets indicate patches to be joined together first before being pieced to the next shape.) Press all seams to one side as you go:
Section 1: Join (AF+Q) to (AI+V) to (W+U) to (K+AG).
Section 2: Join P to E to G to B to J.
Section 3: Join (AB+AJ) to (AC+X) to H to A to F to (R+S) to (AH+T).
Section 4: Join O to D to I to C to L.
Section 5: Join (AE+N) to (Y+AA) to (Z+AK) to (M+AD).
Then join each section to make a block.
Repeat until you have 25 blocks.

5 Join the blocks by stitching them right sides together in rows of five (*fig 3*). Press the seams to one side as you go. Then join the rows together until the patchwork is complete.

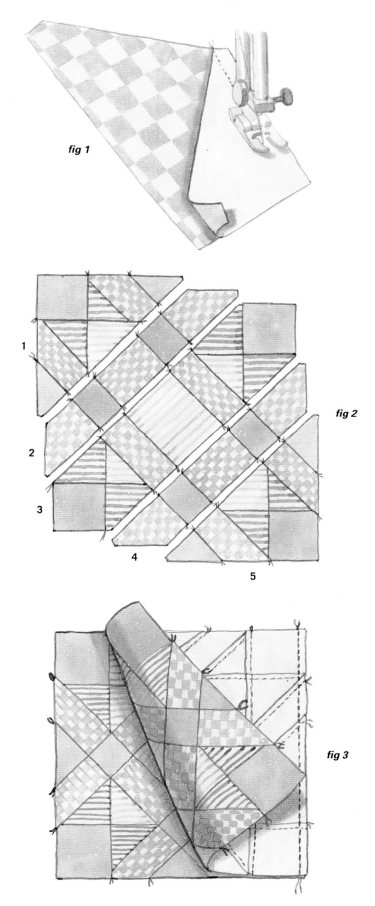

fig 1

fig 2

fig 3

6 Trace off the templates given for the Roman numerals (left) onto the paper side of the fabric bond. The numerals V and the X are shown reversed, the I is symmetrical. You will need 9 of numeral X, 7 of numeral V and 14 of numeral I, i.e. 30 numerals in all.

7 Iron the fabric bond onto the reverse of the woven gold lamé and trim carefully around each shape. Following the photograph below, iron each numeral in the appropriate place on the patchwork.

8 Set up the sewing machine for a narrow satin stitch. Using the metallic gold machine embroidery thread, work satin stitch around all the numerals to neaten the raw edges of the lamé (*fig 4*). As you finish each numeral, pull the thread ends through to the back of the work and knot to secure them. Press.

Templates for the Roman numerals. The V and X are shown reversed.

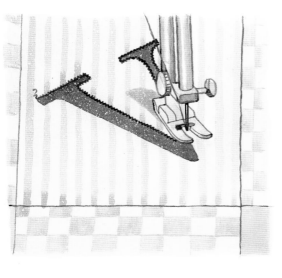

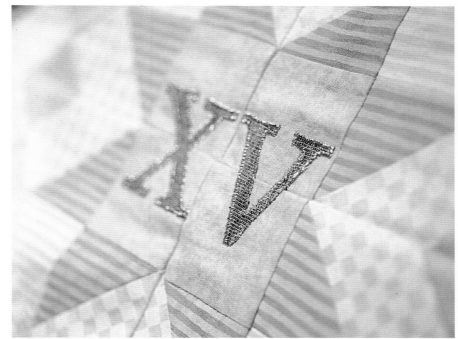

fig 4

9 From the textured beige fabric, cut two border strips 6.5cm (2½in) wide and the length of the finished patchwork cloth. Cut two more border strips 6.5cm (2½in) wide and the finished length plus 12cm (4¾in). With right sides facing, sew the two shorter strips to opposite sides of the patchwork cloth, taking a 6mm (¼in) seam allowance. Press the border flat. Now sew on the two longer border strips in the same way (*fig 5*).

10 Lay the patchwork cloth onto the backing fabric with wrong sides together. The backing fabric should be 1.5cm (⅝in) smaller all around; trim it if necessary. Pin all layers together with quilters' safety pins.

11 The tablecloth now needs to be 'tied' at regular intervals so that it does not distort in use. To achieve this, stitch 'in the ditch' (see page 131) around the large squares that have been formed by the dark textured stone patches. Pull all thread ends through to the back and knot them securely.

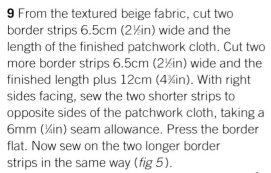

fig 5

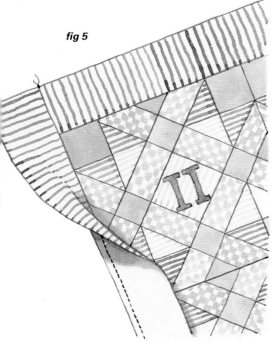

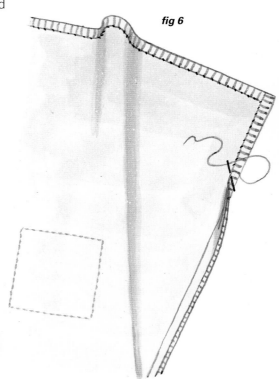

fig 6

12 Turn under the raw edges of the border strips by 5mm (³⁄₁₆in). Then turn under another 1cm (⅜in) and slip stitch in place so that the pressed seam hides the raw edge of the backing fabric (*fig 6*). The border should have a finished width of about 4.5cm (1¾in) on the top of the patchwork cloth.

Cathedral Window Cushion

The colours of stained glass windows lend themselves to the traditional technique of Cathedral Window patchwork, a method of hand piecing and decorative folding. Instead of flat cottons, which tend to absorb the light, silk and voile are used to make this cushion, enhancing the design with their reflective qualities and translucent sheen. Tiny details are added with rouleau tubes coiled into decorative 'roses'. Although the patchwork is all hand-stitched, the cushion itself can be made up on a sewing machine.

Materials and Equipment

- 114 x 100cm (45 x 40in) emerald dupion silk
- 114 x 50cm (45 x 20in) blue/green shot dupion silk
- 60 x 10cm (23½ x 4in) cerise voile
- 50 x 10cm (20 x 4in) rose voile
- 25 x 10cm (10 x 4in) wine voile
- Strong sewing thread in dark grey or to match fabrics
- Sewing thread in blue and green
- Sewing machine (optional)
- Rotary cutter and mat (optional)
- Transparent grid ruler
- Rouleau turner or fine crochet hook
- 5mm (³⁄₁₆in) bias bar
- 36 x 36cm (14 x 14in) cushion pad
- Iron
- Basic sewing kit (see page 120)

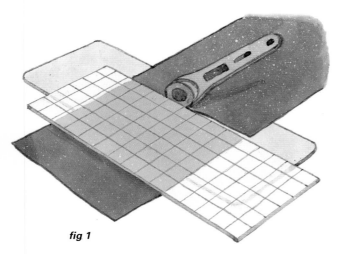

fig 1

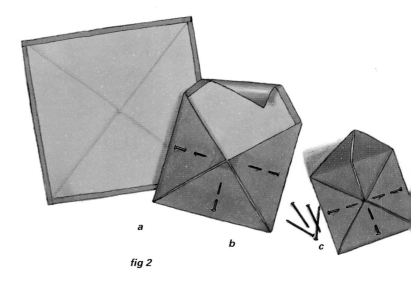

a

b

c

fig 2

Method

1 From the emerald silk, cut five squares measuring 20.3 x 20.3cm (8 x 8in) on the straight grain (*fig 1*). As it is important to cut accurately, it would be helpful to use a rotary cutter, mat and ruler (see page 120). In the same way, cut four squares measuring 20.3 x 20.3cm (8 x 8in) from the blue/green shot silk.

2 On each of the squares, press the raw edges to the wrong side by 6mm (¼in). Then lightly press the squares diagonally each way to mark the centre point (*fig 2a*). Fold all four corners into the centre, working as precisely as possible to avoid problems when joining the squares together (*fig 2b*). Pin in place. Fold the corners into the centre once again and pin in place (*fig 2c*). Press the squares lightly so that they hold their shape for ease of construction.

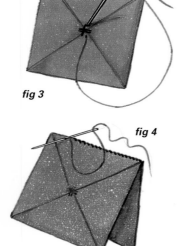

fig 3

fig 4

3 Knot the end of a matching or a dark grey strong sewing thread and sew a double cross stitch through the centre of each patchwork block, securing all layers (*fig 3*). Knot the thread on the reverse to fasten off, as the back will not be seen in this project. Complete all the blocks in this way. Remove the pins.

4 Starting with an emerald block in the top left-hand corner, lay out the blocks alternately to form a chequerboard pattern. With wrong sides together, join two adjacent blocks by oversewing along the top folds with tiny stitches, using a matching or a dark grey thread (*fig 4*). Open out the two blocks and press flat. Continue to sew the blocks together into rows of three, then join the three rows.

5 The 'windows' are made from 5.7 x 5.7cm (2¼ x 2¼in) squares of voile. Some of the squares are cut diagonally to make triangles for the half blocks around the edge of the design. Cut the voile as follows: six full squares plus six triangles in cerise; four full squares plus four triangles in rose; two full squares plus two triangles in wine.

6 Pin the square patches of voile over the pieced blocks, covering the seams where the blocks are joined. Follow the photograph on page 44 for the colour arrangement. Roll back the open edges of the blocks over the raw edges of the square voile patches and slipstitch or stab stitch to secure, using either a blue or green sewing thread as appropriate (*fig 5*).

fig 5

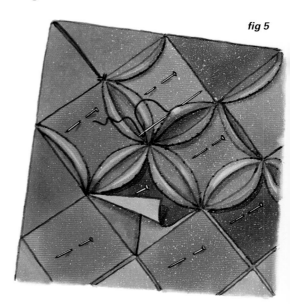

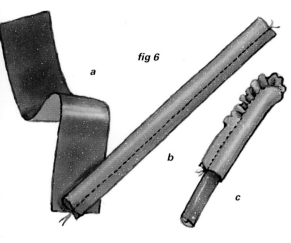

fig 6

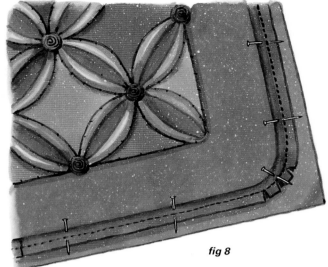

fig 8

7 Add the voile side triangles to the pieced blocks in the same way. Fold the remaining raw edges of the voile to the back of the panel and slip stitch to secure.

8 From the emerald silk, cut a piece measuring 39 x 39cm (15⅜ x 15⅜in) for the cushion front. Pin and slip stitch the patchwork panel centrally to the cushion front.

9 To make the rouleau decoration, cut bias strips of blue/green and emerald silk measuring 2cm (¾in) wide and 10cm (4in) long (fig 6a). You will need 13 lengths of blue/green and 8 lengths of emerald. Fold each strip in half lengthways and stitch along the long edge, taking a 5mm (³⁄₁₆in) seam allowance (fig 6b). Turn the tube right side out using a rouleau turner or a fine crochet hook (fig 6c). Press the rouleau flat with the seam along the lower edge, using a 5mm (³⁄₁₆in) bias bar as a guide.

10 Roll each rouleau into a 'rose' shape by coiling it tightly, tucking the raw edge under. Hand stitch from underneath to prevent it coming loose (fig 7). Sew a rose with small, neat stitches to the centre of each patchwork block where the folded-back edges of the silk meet. Use the photograph on page 44 as a placement guide.

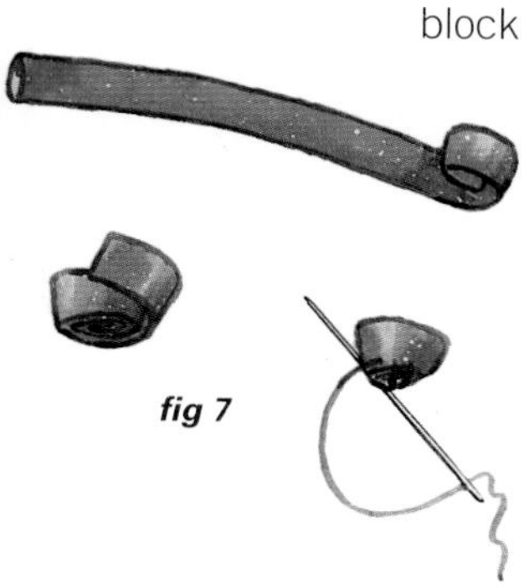

11 To make the trim for the cushion, cut a bias strip from the blue/green silk 1.5cm (⅝in) wide and 150cm (59in) long (joining short lengths together where necessary). Fold the strip in half lengthways with wrong sides together and stitch, taking a 5mm (³⁄₁₆in) seam allowance. Pin the trim all around the cushion front, curving it around and clipping the raw edges at the corners. The raw edge should face the raw edge of the cushion and the stitching line should lie on the cushion seam line, 1.5cm (⅝in) from the edge (fig 8). At each end of the trim, tuck the raw edge inside, then butt up the ends where they meet.

12 From the emerald silk, cut two back panels for the cushion, each measuring 39 x 24cm (15⅜ x 9½in). Fold under a 1cm (⅜in) turning and press. Then fold under another 2cm (¾in) turning and pin. Stitch along the folded edge with a matching sewing thread. Repeat for the second back panel. With right sides together, lay the two panels on top of the cushion front, overlapping them so that they fit the cushion. Pin in place (fig 9) and baste. Stitch around the outside edge taking a 1.5cm (⅝in) seam allowance, making sure that you catch in the edge of the trim as you stitch. Remove the basting thread, trim the excess fabric from the corners and turn right side out. Insert the cushion pad.

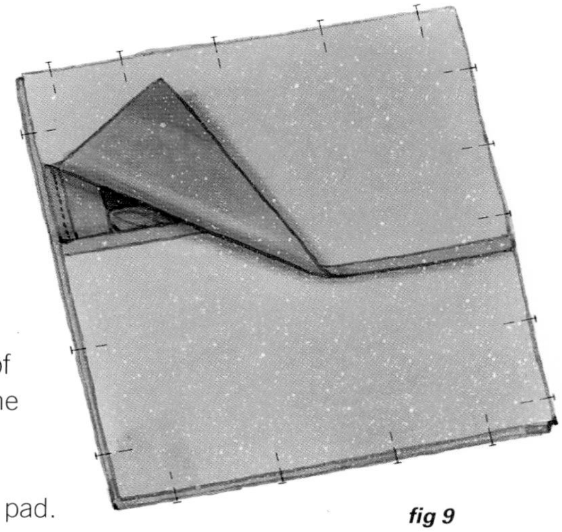

fig 7

fig 9

Seminole Tie-back

The colour scheme in this tie-back was inspired by photographs of terracotta tiles taken in Florence in Italy and incorporates some of the rich variety of reds and oranges to be seen in them. A purple shade has been introduced to break up the other colours and to provide a subtle contrast to them. The Seminole patchwork technique used for the tie-back is based on joining long strips of fabric, then cutting and rearranging these to create geometric patterns. The unusual zigzag trim is made with Somerset points.

Materials and Equipment
(*for two tie-backs*)
- 'Fat quarters' of cotton fabric (see page 142) in the following hand-dyed colours: orange, pink, wine, variegated orange, purple
- Dark orange sewing thread
- Sewing machine
- Rotary cutter and mat
- Transparent grid ruler
- Rouleau turner or small safety pin
- Iron
- Basic sewing kit (see page 120)

Method

1 In order to give your tie-back an interesting marbled effect, either hand-dye your fabrics (see page 137) or buy variegated fabrics from a specialist supplier.

2 Using a rotary cutter, mat and ruler (see page 120) and following the fabric grain, cut enough strips from the 'fat quarters' of fabric to make one tie-back. First, cut one pink and one purple border strip, each measuring 3.5 x 52cm (1⅜in x 20½in). Then, for the Seminole patchwork, cut two strips right across the fat quarters in each of the following colours and widths: orange 2.25cm (⅞in); pink and purple 3.2cm (1¼in); wine and variegated orange 3.5cm (1⅜in). Finally, cut 13 strips from the orange fabric for the Somerset points, each measuring 3.2 x 5cm (1¼ x 2in).

3 Set up your sewing machine for straight stitch (stitch length 2). All the seam allowances in this project are 5mm (³⁄₁₆in). Using dark orange thread, sew the strips together in two groups of five, in the following order: wine, pink, orange, purple, variegated (*fig 1*). Trim any ragged edges at top and bottom and press all the seam allowances to one side.

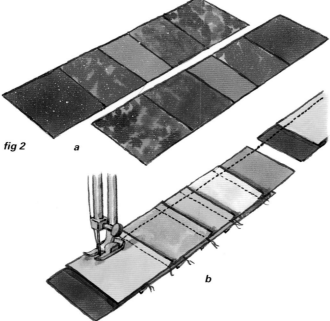

fig 1

fig 2   **a**

b

4 Cut strips 3.8cm (1½in) wide from the pieced fabric, cutting across all five colours. These strips are now sewn together in pairs to begin creating the Seminole pattern. To achieve the correct diagonal pattern for the tie-back, turn one strip of each pair the opposite way round to the other and offset it by one orange block (*fig 2a*). You can chain-sew the pairs of strips on the sewing machine to save time (*fig 2b*), cutting the linking threads afterwards (see page 142).

5 Now sew all the pairs to each other, arranging them so that they continue to form the diagonal pattern as described in step 4, until the Seminole patchwork measures approximately 56cm (22in). You will need nine pairs for one tie-back. Press the seam allowances to one side.

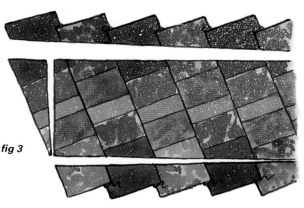

fig 3

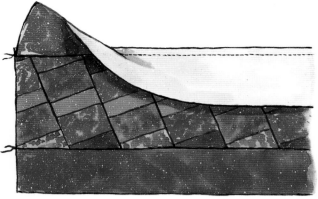

fig 4

6 Using the rotary cutter and ruler, trim off the excess fabric on each side of the patchwork strip in order to create straight edges, leaving a 5mm (³⁄₁₆in) seam allowance all around (*fig 3*).

7 Take the two border strips and pin the pink strip along the top edge of the patchwork and the purple strip along the lower edge. Stitch and press (*fig 4*).

8 Make the Somerset points from the 13 small strips of orange fabric. Fold under a narrow turning along one edge of the first strip (*fig 5a*). Fold the rectangle in half and finger press to mark the midline. Fold each top corner to the base of the midline to make a triangle (*fig 5b*). Repeat for all the strips.

9 Lay the triangles right sides down along the purple border, overlapping them slightly and with their points facing towards the centre. Leave the seam allowance free at each end. Pin and baste in place (*fig 6*). Cut a lining from one of the excess fat quarters to match the size of the tie-back.

10 Lay the tie-back and lining right sides together and sew along the top and bottom edges. Stitch one short side, too, but leave a 1cm (³⁄₈in) gap at the top. Trim the excess fabric at the corners, turn right side out and press. Fold in the raw edges of the open side, press and slip stitch, leaving a 1cm (³⁄₈in) gap at the top as before.

11 Make hanging loops by cutting two pink strips each measuring 2 x 10cm (¾ x 4in). Fold the strips lengthways with right sides together and stitch. Turn them to the right side using a rouleau turner or safety pin. Press each one, then fold into a loop. Insert the raw ends into the gaps left in the side seams of the

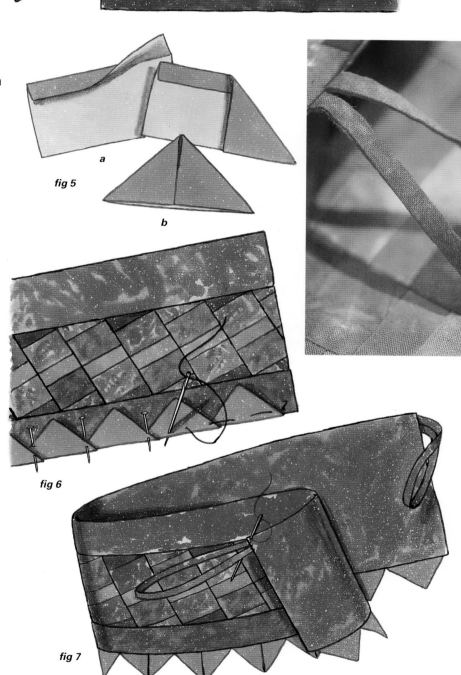

fig 5

a

b

fig 6

fig 7

tie-back and stitch in place (*fig 7*). Repeat the making up instructions from step 2 to make a second tie-back.

sea and sky

Above: *The simplicity of this close-up view of driftwood could be expressed in trapunto or shadow quilting, or as an unusual pieced block.*
Opposite page: top left – *Never underestimate the sky as a source of vibrant colour contrasts, as this picture demonstrates well;*
top right – *A tropical fish in vivid shades forms a classic image for quilting, appliqué or stylized piecing;*
below left – *Overlapping starfish make an attractive repeat pattern for shadow quilting or hand quilting;*
below right – *Try interpreting a photograph of the sea in strip piecing, perhaps adding some embroidery to suggest light on the water.*

The sea and the ever-changing sky above it provide a rich source of design ideas for patchwork and quilting, not always obvious ones. The activities associated with the seaside will spark off ideas too.

A trip to the seaside is always an enjoyable day out with plenty to capture your interest. Yachts sailing past or moored in a marina offer both colour and repeat patterns within their hulls and sails which are ideal for simple block piecing. Alternatively, look for bright colours and shapes in the stalls that often line the sea front – the gaily hued buckets and spades or sticks of rock present varied patches of colour. Take close-up photographs of any eye-catching details, isolating the areas that you like best. These will inspire you later when you translate your ideas into designs on paper before commencing fabric sampling.

For lively quilting patterns, look at the texture of spray chasing over the crest of a wave. This suggests to me densely textured quilting next to areas of sparser lines. For even more texture, clusters of shells clinging to rocks could be interpreted in raised trapunto quilting. Wherever you live, you can sketch or photograph the sky during all the seasons. From these you can build up a palette of colour-washed hues inspired by the clouds, perfect to translate into a subtle log cabin design with free machine quilting. Instead of taking designs directly from nature, another source of ideas is reproductions of old mariners' maps. Look for interesting lines and motifs where the sea meets the land and interpret these in strip patchwork and appliqué. For extra effect, incorporate lettering into the project with embroidery stitches.

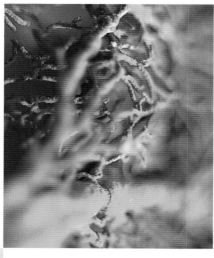

Right – *This coral formation suggests a meandering quilt pattern as well as offering a contrasting colour palette.*
Below – *The gossamer appearance of the pale coral would look superb in shadow quilted sheers, using metallic threads for highlights.*

Opposite page: top – *Sometimes it is interesting to try to recreate an image faithfully. This tranquil seascape could be strip pieced, appliquéd and embellished with hand embroidery;*
below left – *This three-dimensional view of coral would be striking worked in trapunto quilting;*
below right – *A muted palette such as the one created by these rusty, lichen-encrusted chains would make a project look very sophisticated.*

Left – An anchor is a bold, immediately recognizable image that would make a good border design in navy, white and red.
Right – The effect of repeating the same object at different scales is shown by this detail of polished pebbles. Quilt spirals in varying sizes to create the pattern.

Opposite page – These divided wooden boxes filled with a wonderful variety of shells could be effectively recreated with quilted blocks pieced together with contrasting sashings.

Left – A beautiful, timeless and delicate image is provided by the sea horse. Use its outline for shadow or machine quilting.

Left – Translate the spine markings on this sea urchin into squares of varying sizes on grid paper and colour them in as inspiration for a geometric design.
Right – Twisted cords and fine rope in neutral colours make ideal tassels and trims for nautically inspired throws and cushions.

Crazy Patchwork Quilt

The colour scheme of this exuberant quilt was inspired by tropical fish. The irregular-shaped patches are covered in machine embroidery and have been stuffed separately to give a contoured surface and extra softness. Hang the quilt on the wall as a showpiece or use it as a sofa throw or to cover a toddler's bed. If you use it for a child, you may prefer to make it from brightly coloured cottons for practicality.

Materials and Equipment
- 45 x 114cm (18 x 45in) dupion silk in each of gold/pink shot, pink, lilac, orange, dark green, pale blue
- 45 x 45cm (18 x 18in) pale green dupion silk
- Oddments of dupion silk in red, beige, lime green, purple
- 87.5 x 114cm (35 x 45in) white cotton backing fabric
- 87.5 x 114cm (35 x 45in) lining fabric to match
- 54 x 120cm (21 x 47in) fusible fabric bond
- Loose quilt batting or shredded wadding
- Anchor machine embroidery threads: one reel in each of gold 2724, lilac 2463, pink 2334, pale green 2639, dark green 2667, orange 2285, pale blue 2521
- Sewing machine
- Dressmaker's pattern paper or grid paper
- Fabric marking pencil or tailor's chalk
- Knitting needle
- Embroidery hoop
- Iron
- Basic sewing kit (see page 120)

Method

1 Using dressmaker's pattern paper or grid paper, enlarge the templates given on the cutting layouts on pages 65-67. Place them onto the appropriate colour of silk as shown and mark around the outlines with fabric marking pencil or tailor's chalk.

Template for all-over shell motif

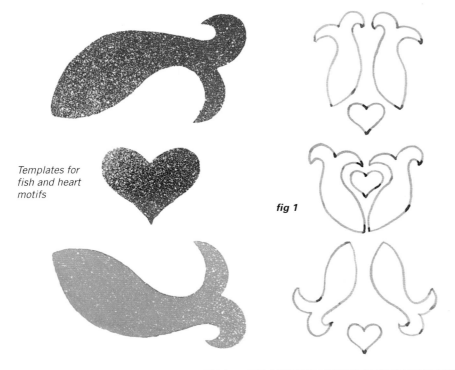

Templates for fish and heart motifs

fig 1

2 Set up the sewing machine for free embroidery (see page 134). Referring to the cutting layouts, embroider the patches labelled vermicelli stitch, straight stitch lines and all-over shells. The template for the all-over shell motif is shown above. Check the detail photograph on page 64 to see which colours of machine embroidery thread to use or choose your own combination of colours.

3 Trace the fish and heart motifs (left) onto the paper side of the fabric bond. Iron onto the back of the silk oddments and cut out. Bond to the 'kissing fish' patches, placing them in the arrangements shown in *fig 1*. Work the details and scrolled lines with free machine embroidery. N.B. Instead of machine embroidery, you could use simple hand-embroidery stitches. Similarly, you could substitute textured fabric for the patches covered in all-over machine embroidery.

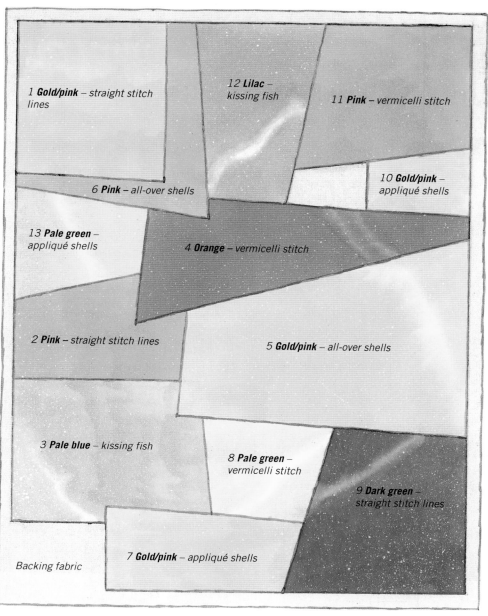

1 **Gold/pink** – straight stitch lines

12 **Lilac** – kissing fish

11 **Pink** – vermicelli stitch

6 **Pink** – all-over shells

10 **Gold/pink** – appliqué shells

13 **Pale green** – appliqué shells

4 **Orange** – vermicelli stitch

2 **Pink** – straight stitch lines

5 **Gold/pink** – all-over shells

3 **Pale blue** – kissing fish

8 **Pale green** – vermicelli stitch

9 **Dark green** – straight stitch lines

7 **Gold/pink** – appliqué shells

Backing fabric

fig 2

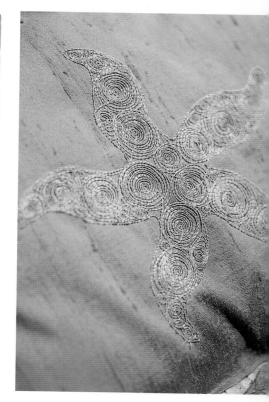

4 Once all large patches have been embroidered, cut them out. Also cut out the patches that will have shells appliquéd to them. Turn the raw edges under, trimming the pointed corners first. Pin the patches onto the backing fabric in the order given in *fig 2*. Overlap each patch slightly to hide the backing fabric. Machine stitch them in place using the appropriate colour of machine embroidery thread.

5 Trace the starfish motif (right) onto the appropriate patches and embroider by hand or machine. Cut out the patches, turn under the edges and sew in place on the quilt.

Template for starfish motif

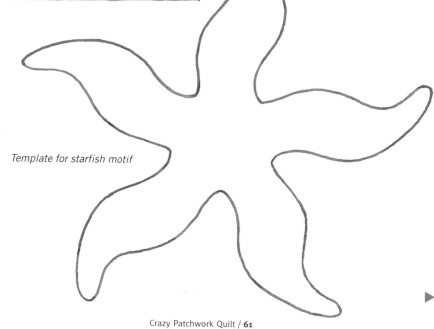

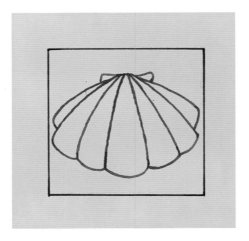

Templates for the appliqué shell motifs

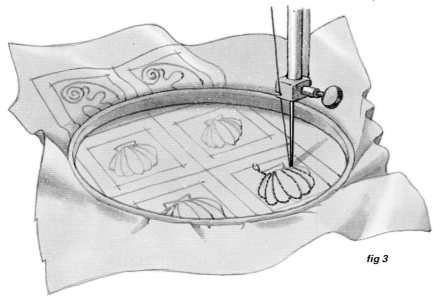

fig 3

6 Trace and embroider the appliqué shell motifs (above) on the remaining gold/pink shot silk, changing the thread colour as you wish in order to create highlights (*fig 3*). This type of machine embroidery is expressive, rather like 'painting' with thread. Trim the fabric into small squares and fringe the edges (see page 142). Sew the squares onto the quilt with straight stitch.

7 Fuse fabric bond onto the back of the wave shapes on the dark green and lilac silk. Cut them out. Bond them onto the quilt (*fig 4*), following the detail photograph on page 64. Embellish with continuous spiral machine embroidery, using a variety of thread colours.

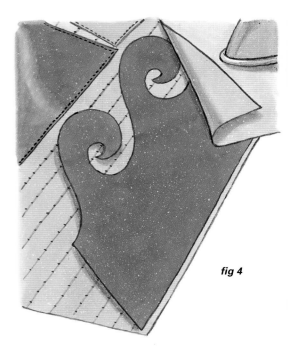

fig 4

8 Once all the patches are embroidered, turn the quilt over and make small slits in the backing fabric under each patch except for the waves. Stuff the patches individually, pushing the batting in with a knitting needle (see trapunto quilting on page 132).

9 Trim any uneven edges around the quilt and lay it onto the lining fabric with wrong sides together. Baste around the edges. Cut four strips from the orange silk for the binding, as shown on the cutting layout. Press the binding in half lengthways and press the raw edges under by 5mm (³⁄₁₆in) on each side (*fig 5*).

10 Lay a strip of binding along one short edge of the quilt 1cm (³⁄₈in) in from the edge and stitch along the pressed line (*fig 6a*). Fold over to the back of the quilt and slip stitch in place (*fig 6b*). Repeat for the other short edge, then the long edges. At the corners where the bindings meet, overlap them and turn the short raw edges under to hide them (*fig 6c*). Press around the edges to finish.

fig 5

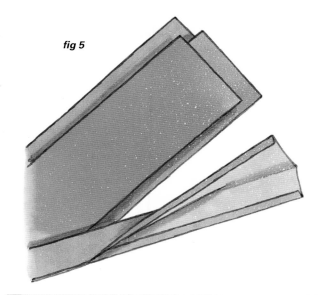

fig 6

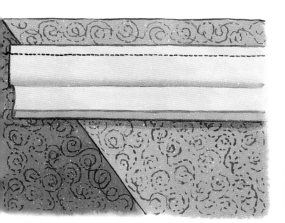

a

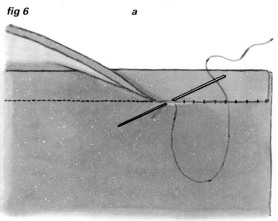

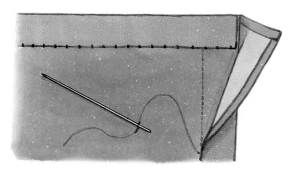

b

c

Gold/pink shot dupion silk

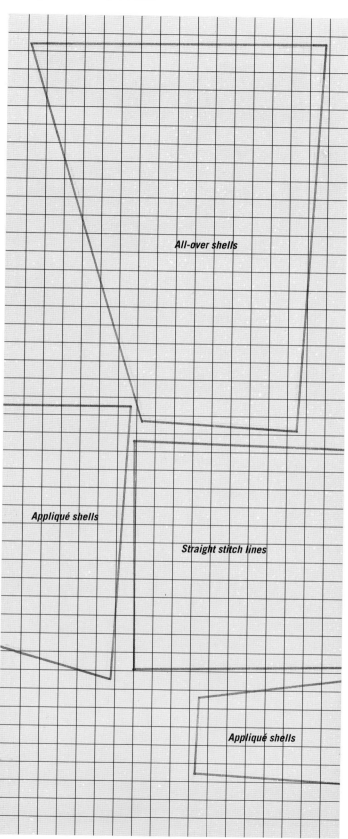

All-over shells

Appliqué shells

Straight stitch lines

Appliqué shells

Pink dupion silk

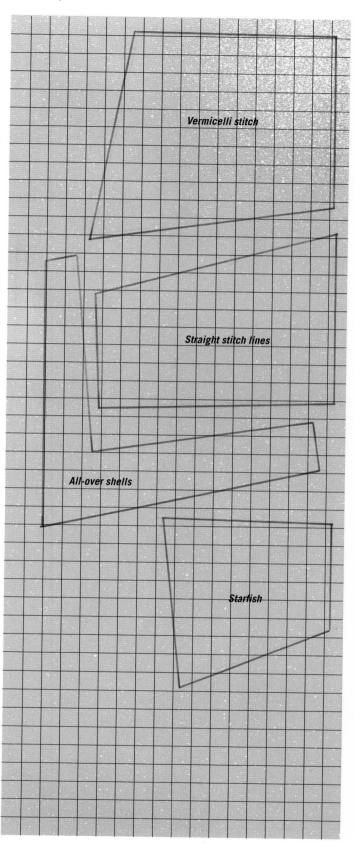

Vermicelli stitch

Straight stitch lines

All-over shells

Starfish

Cutting layouts for the silk patches.
Each square = 2.5 x 2.5cm (1 x 1in).

Dark green dupion silk

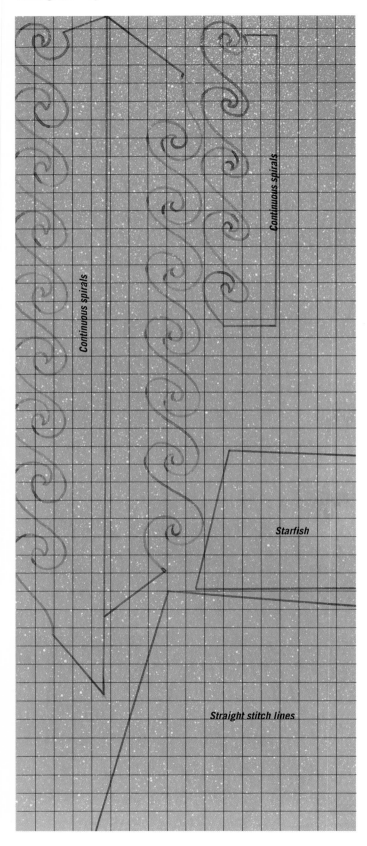

Continuous spirals

Continuous spirals

Starfish

Straight stitch lines

Pale blue dupion silk

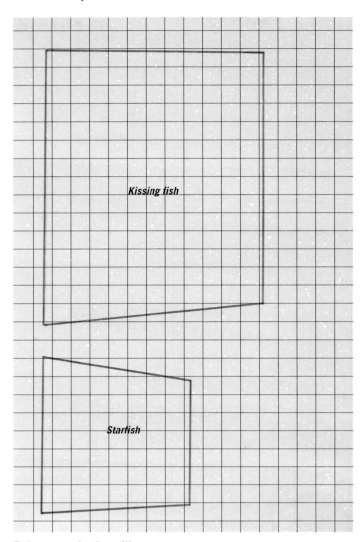

Kissing fish

Starfish

Pale green dupion silk

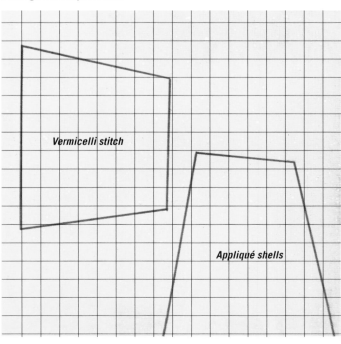

Vermicelli stitch

Appliqué shells

Lilac dupion silk

Orange dupion silk

Continuous spirals

Continuous spirals

Starfish

Kissing fish

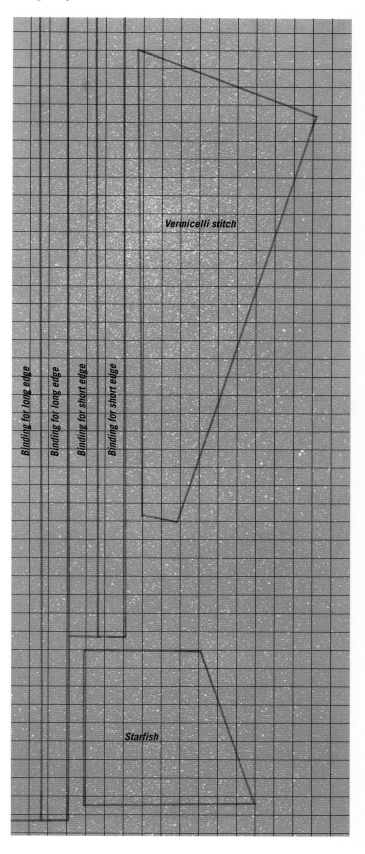

Vermicelli stitch

Binding for long edge

Binding for long edge

Binding for short edge

Binding for short edge

Starfish

Cutting layouts for the silk patches.
Each square = 2.5 x 2.5cm (1 x 1in).

Stratos Washbag

This simple washbag was inspired by the colours of the sky and by cloud formations in all their variety. The fabric was dyed to represent a range of skies, from a clear summery blue with wispy clouds to a dark, stormy indigo. The patchwork technique used is straightforward piecing and quilting. Although the bag illustrated has been machine-pieced, it can easily be worked by hand, making it an ideal project to take when travelling or on holiday.

Materials and Equipment

- 'Fat quarters' (see page 142) of the following cotton fabrics: random-dyed bright blue, mid blue and dark blue; white-on-white print
- 35 x 100cm (14 x 40in) pre-quilted towelling
- 2m (2⅛yd) white cotton bias binding, 2cm (¾in) wide
- 1m (1⅛yd) blue cord
- White sewing thread
- Sewing machine
- Rotary cutter and mat
- Transparent grid ruler
- Quilters' safety pins (optional)
- Iron
- Basic sewing kit (see page 120)

Method

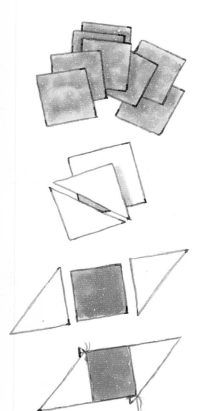

1 If you wish to dye your own cotton fabrics for the sky colours, see page 137. Otherwise, substitute patterned fabrics in three shades of blue. From the fat quarters, cut out the strips for the horizontal bands around the bag, using the rotary cutter, mat and ruler. You will need two strips of each colour and size specified: sky blue 5 x 28.5cm (2 x 11¼in); mid blue 2 x 28.5cm (¾ x 11¼in) and 3 x 28.5cm (1¼ x 11¼in); dark blue 2 x 28.5cm (¾ x 11¼in) and 5 x 28.5cm (2 x 11¼in). Join the strips in pairs to make up the full length. Take a 5mm (³⁄₁₆in) seam allowance throughout.

2 Cut ten 5 x 5cm (2 x 2in) squares from each of the three shades of blue cotton. Cut 33 squares measuring 6 x 6cm (2⅜ x 2⅜in) from the white-on-white printed cotton. Cut the white squares in half diagonally to make triangles.

3 Take one sky blue square and machine stitch two white triangles to opposite sides of it, making a parallelogram shape (*fig 1*). Stitch two triangles to opposite sides of the remaining sky blue squares in the same way, using the chain stitch method if you wish (see page 142).

4 Take two of the stitched sections and join them together along one long edge. The squares will begin to make a diamond formation (*fig 2*). Join all the other sections together to make a strip of sky blue diamonds.

fig 1

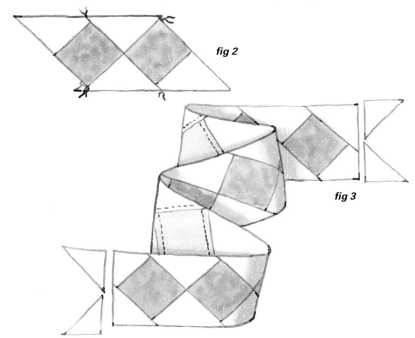

fig 2

fig 3

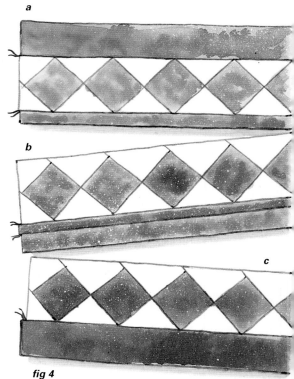

a

b

c

fig 4

5 At each end of the strip, add an extra white triangle in order to give enough width for a seam allowance. Trim the side edges straight, leaving at least a 5mm (³⁄₁₆in) seam allowance beyond the outer sky blue diamonds (*fig 3*). Repeat steps 3, 4 and 5 for the mid and dark blue squares. Press all seam allowances in the same direction.

6 Now stitch all the strips together to make the bag, following the piecing order given in *fig 4*.
a) Join the 5cm (2in) wide sky blue strip to the top edge of the sky blue diamond strip. Then join the 2cm (¾in) wide mid blue strip to the lower edge of the sky blue diamond strip.
b) Join the dark blue 2cm (¾in) wide strip to the mid blue 3cm (1¼in) wide strip. Then join these two strips to the bottom of the mid blue diamond strip.
c) Join the dark blue diamond strip to the 5cm (2in) wide dark blue strip.
You now have three wide bands of different-coloured diamonds. Stitch the sky blue diamond band to the mid blue diamond band, then add the dark blue diamond band. Press all seam allowances in the same direction. The finished size is now approximately 56 x 29cm (22 x 11½in).

7 From the quilted towelling cut a circle 17.5cm (6⅞in) in diameter for the base. Then lay the patchwork on top of the remaining quilted towelling, wrong sides together. The towelling will be larger all round. Pin in place using quilters' safety pins or baste the layers together with a grid of stitches ready for quilting (*fig 5*).

8 If your machine has a dual feed foot, a walking foot or a quilting foot, use one of these to make the quilting easier. Set the stitch length to 5; the stitches need to be quite long, otherwise they will 'drag' the layers of fabric and look uneven. In any case, long stitches look much smaller when used for quilting than for a normal seam.

9 Begin by stitching 'in the ditch' of all the seams joining the strips (see page 131). (Start and finish the stitching line for the sky blue strip 5mm (³⁄₁₆in) in from the ends, as it will form part of the cord casing in step 10.) Reverse stitch at each end of the stitching lines or pull the thread ends through to the back and knot them. Quilt the white triangles with simple wavy lines, following the detail photograph below. Trim the excess towelling from around the patchwork.

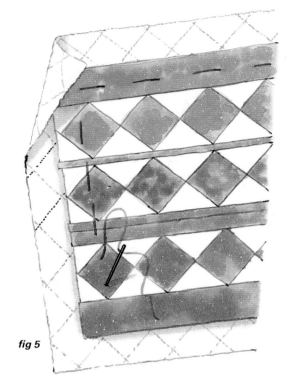

fig 5

10 To make a casing for the cord, stitch a line on the sky blue strip 1cm (⅜in) up from the seamline, starting and finishing 5mm (³⁄₁₆in) in from the ends. This will create a channel for the cord to be pulled through (*fig 6*).

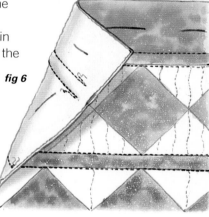

fig 6

11 Fold the bag in half right sides together to join the side seam. Taking a 5mm (³⁄₁₆in) seam allowance, stitch up to the cord casing, but do not stitch across it. Continue stitching above the casing to the top. Thread the cord through the casing. As you are doing this, push the raw edges of the sky blue fabric into the opening of the casing to neaten them, but leave the towelling seam free. (This is rather fiddly.) Stitch bias binding over the raw seam edge, taking care not to catch in the cord (*fig 7*).

12 Cut a circle 17.5cm (6⅞in) in diameter from the dark blue fabric and lay it wrong sides together on the circular towelling base. Baste them together. Insert the base into the main part of the bag, pinning and easing in before basting. Try not to make any gathers or folds. Machine stitch the base in place, taking a 5mm (³⁄₁₆in) seam allowance. Cover the raw seam with bias binding. Turn the bag right side out. Finish by edging the top of the bag with bias binding. Tie knots in the cord ends to prevent them fraying.

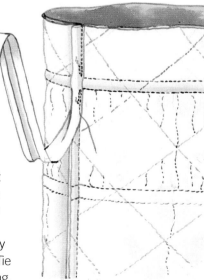

fig 7

Cot Quilt With Yacht

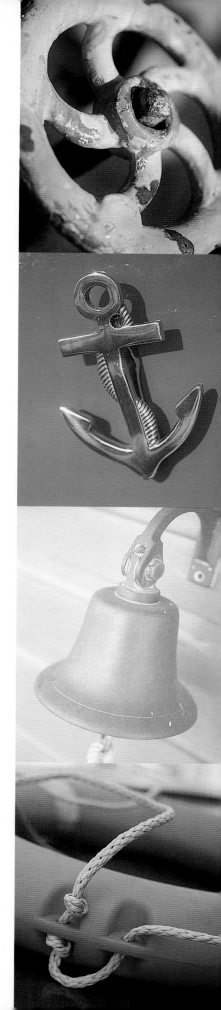

Traditional cottons such as denim, chambray and gingham in fresh blue and white give this cosy child's quilt an appealing homespun quality. Red polka dot fabric is used as a contrast. A yacht motif has been appliquéd onto the centre of the quilt to give a nautical theme, but any simple motif, perhaps a car, a flower or a teddy, would be equally suitable.

Materials and Equipment

- 35 x 114cm (13¾ x 45in) cotton fabric in each of the following colours: blue denim, blue chambray, large blue gingham check, small blue gingham check, blue polka dot, white
- 120 x 114cm (48 x 45in) red polka dot cotton fabric
- 80 x 98cm (31½ x 38½in) 113g (4oz) wadding
- 22 x 20cm (8¾ x 8in) fusible fabric bond
- Sewing thread in white or mid blue
- Anchor machine embroidery thread: one reel in gold 2110
- Sewing machine
- Rotary cutter and mat
- Transparent grid ruler
- Quilters' safety pins
- Iron
- Basic sewing kit (see page 120)

Method

1 Using the rotary cutter, mat and ruler (see page 120), first cut strips for the striped border. You will need to cut one strip 5.5 x 114cm (2⅛ x 45in) from each of the fabrics except the white. To make piecing more efficient, sew the strips together in pairs first, taking a seam allowance of 5mm (³⁄₁₆in) (*fig 1*). Then join the pairs together until the finished piece measures approximately 28 x 114cm (11 x 45in). Press the seams to one side. Cut the piece widthways into 10cm (3⅞in) strips and lay them to one side.

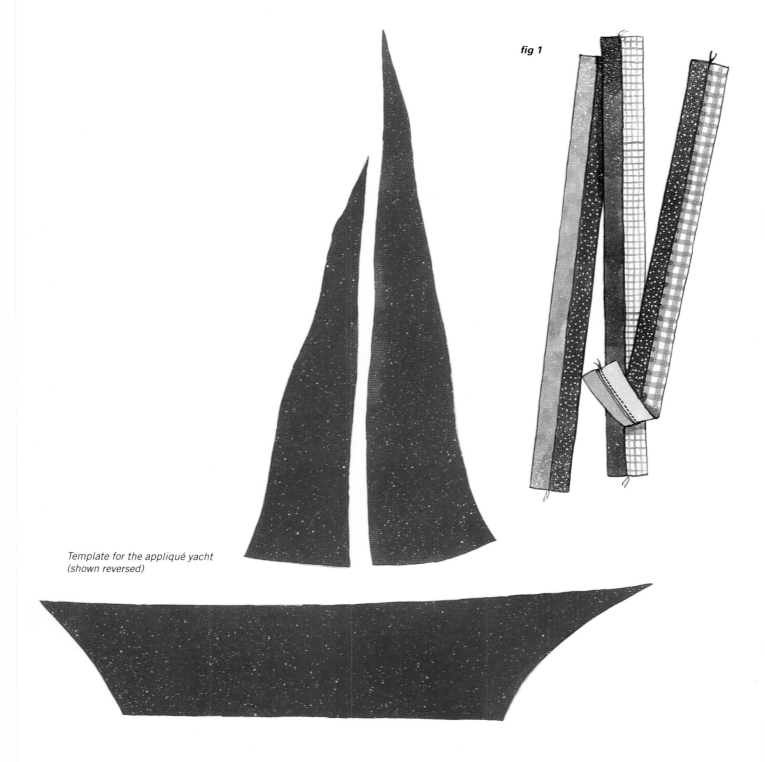

fig 1

Template for the appliqué yacht (shown reversed)

fig 2　　　　　　　　　　**fig 3**

2 Each square patch for the main part of the quilt measures 10 x 10cm (3⅞ x 3⅞in). You will need to cut the following number of patches in the colours specified: 12 in denim (including the four corners), 12 in chambray, 10 in large gingham check, 13 in small gingham check, 12 in blue polka dot, 8 in white. This will give a total of 67 squares.

3 Lay out the patches in the correct arrangement for the quilt and begin to sew them together to form horizontal strips (*fig 2*). Take a 5mm (³⁄₁₆in) seam allowance throughout. Press the seams to one side. When all nine horizontal strips are complete, join them together row by row. Press the seams to one side.

4 Trace the yacht template (opposite) onto the paper side of the fusible fabric bond. From the red polka dot fabric, cut a piece 22 x 20cm (8¾ x 8in). Iron the bond onto the reverse of the fabric and cut out the motif (*fig 3*). Place it centrally onto the quilt top and iron in place.

5 Set up the sewing machine for free embroidery (see page 134). Using gold machine embroidery thread, embroider the details on the yacht motif as shown in the detail photograph (right). Reset the machine for straight stitch.

6 To make the borders, join the strips already made in step 1 to fit the side, top and bottom edges of the quilt (*fig 4a*). Add a denim square to each end of the top and bottom strips to form corners (*fig 4b*).

7 With right sides together, first sew the side border strips in place. As one square patch on the quilt is equal to two of the border patches, try to match up the seams for a neat finish. Press the side seams open. Then sew on the top and bottom border strips. The finished top should measure approximately 80 x 98cm (31½ x 38½in).

8 Cut out a piece of red polka dot fabric measuring 92 x 110cm (36¼ x 43¼in) for the quilt backing. Layer the backing with the piece of wadding and the patchwork to make a quilt sandwich (see page 130). Use quilters' safety pins to hold all the layers together before quilting, pinning through the seam every second square along (*fig 5*).

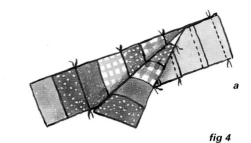

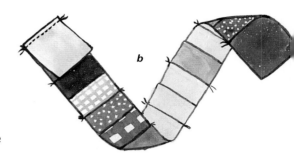

fig 4

a

b

fig 5

9 Set the stitch length on the sewing machine to 4 and use a dual feed foot, a walking foot or a quilting foot. Begin to quilt 'in the ditch' (see page 131) around the light blue centre panel. Continue to quilt 'in the ditch', working from the centre outwards around each 'frame' of patches. Lastly, quilt the seam between the border and the quilt top. All seams should be quilted in the same direction to avoid puckering the fabric (*fig 6*).

10 Trim away any excess wadding that may be showing around the edges. Trim the red backing fabric down to 4cm (1½in) extra all

around to form a binding. Turn under 1cm (⅜in) all round the backing fabric and press. To mitre each corner, trim off the point (*fig 7a*) and fold the corner onto the quilt top (*fig 7b*). Fold up another 3cm (1⅛in) of the binding, forming a diagonal mitre. Slipstitch the mitred edge in place (*fig 7c*).

11 Fold the remaining binding to the top of the quilt. (The depth of the quilt will take up about 1cm (⅜in), leaving an edging of 2cm (¾in) showing on the front. Pin, then machine stitch the binding in place about 5mm (³⁄₁₆in) in from the edge. Sew up the corner seams.

fig 6

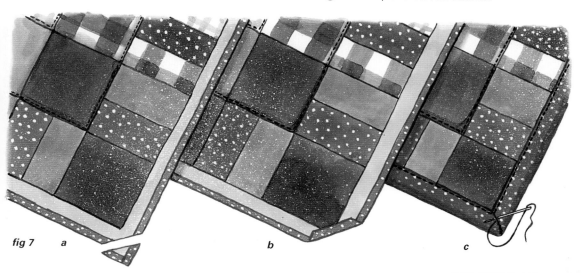

fig 7   a   b   c

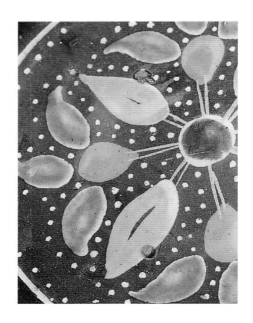

global
and ethnic

Above: This naive hand-painted cloth with its bold, stylized floral image could be interpreted in appliqué together with knotted and tied quilting.
Opposite page: top left – *Painted beads in the brightest of colours create a stimulating image that could be pieced to form a stunning quilt top;*
top right – *Interpret the hand-prints in this fascinating cave painting in a combination of stencilling and quilting;*
below left – *Strong bands of colour set on the slant, as in this feather cloak, suggest Seminole patchwork borders;*
below right – *Rows of corn cobs with their different markings and patterns conjure up strip pieced designs.*

Thanks to improved communications and travel, it is now easier than ever to find unusual sources of inspiration for your own work from many different cultures around the world.

Whether you are a globetrotter or an armchair traveller, you will find endless inspiration for your own work among the arts and crafts of other cultures. Close to home, many cities have areas where particular ethnic groups live and work. Here, it is possible to observe and buy artefacts of genuine origin without having to travel to distant countries. For example, you could collect inexpensive hand-painted boxes and use them to suggest a colour scheme for a quilt. Stacked up, the boxes would create patterns for patchwork blocks or for simple strip patchwork. African carvings and beads have strong shapes that could be developed into motifs for quilting. These would look particularly effective worked on authentic batik silks to make small cushions or accessories. Tiles from Morocco have intensely rich hues of purple and blue against a white background. Their stylized leaf or floral motifs could be simplified into geometric shapes for piecing. It is not just today's ethnic art and crafts that will inspire you. Cultures long since lost, such as the Aztecs and the Incas of South America, continue to influence designers today with their distinctive and original designs. If you are interested in other cultures, there are many books available with beautiful photographs showing the lifestyles of communities around the globe. Treat yourself to a coffee-table book and let your mind soak up the exciting possibilities of a multicultural quilt.

Right – *This cheeky-looking monkey would bring a sense of fun to any project. Hand-paint it and quilt around the outline and features.*
Below – *Heart motifs appear frequently in folk art on all sorts of different objects and still have an everlasting romantic appeal for quilting designs. Stencil hearts in place first, then stitch around them.*

Opposite page: top – *The linear marks of the eye detailed on this punched metal box are alive with possibilities for quilting using machine and hand stitches together with trapunto work;*
below left – *A woven bamboo basket could be the source for interweaving lightly quilted strips of calico to create an unusual curtain tie-back;*
below right – *Glass beads have been set into this textured metal box. Stitch beads in place on quilted garments or opulent throws for extra sparkle.*

Left – A bold leaf printed half and half in positive and negative illustrates a good basic design principle.

Right – The facial decoration on this carved wooden head is a lesson in design in its own right. The neutral colour scheme could be reproduced using natural fabrics.

Opposite page – This gorgeous photograph of shells and feathers presents a sophisticated palette of greys from palest pearl through to pewter. The shapes and muted colours suggest shadow quilting with the sewing machine.

Left – The iridescent colours on this feather tip could only be done justice with rich silks and chiffons machine-pieced and enhanced with machine embroidery using shiny threads.

Left – Stylize this image even further and interpret it in block quilting as a repeating design. Try varying the scale of the blocks for more interest.

Right – A silky tasselled edge like this one could be applied to a lightly quilted throw for a decadent look.

Tribal Cushion

The design for this cushion was influenced by images of African tribal crafts. The tribespeople draw on natural objects for their inspiration and much of their work has a neutral colour palette, especially the wood and stone carvings. An unbleached linen fabric was chosen for the cushion, both for its tactile quality and its subtle colour. The decorations of beads and feathers were gathered from various sources.

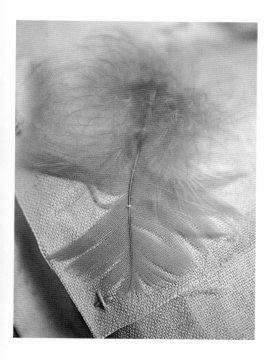

Materials and Equipment
- 60 x 86cm (23½ x 34in) natural linen
- Cream sewing thread
- Cream buttonhole thread
- Four small feathers
- 12 wooden hand-painted beads (similar to large bugle beads)
- Four rectangular stone beads
- Four irregular-shaped pearl beads
- 35 x 35cm (13¾ x 13¾in) cushion pad
- Sewing machine (optional)
- Rotary cutter and mat (optional)
- Transparent grid ruler (optional)
- Iron
- Basic sewing kit (see page 120)

Method

1 From the linen cut out a square 38 x 38cm (15 x 15in) for the cushion front. Cut out two rectangles each 24 x 38cm (9½ x 15in) to make panels for an envelope back.

2 Using a rotary cutter, mat and ruler (see page 120) or scissors, cut out 12 squares from the linen, each measuring 6 x 6cm (2⅜ x 2⅜in). Then cut out four smaller squares, each 3 x 3cm (1¼ x 1¼in). Finally, cut out four larger squares each 9 x 9cm (3½ x 3½in) to make the folded squares.

3 Begin decorating the linen squares. First take four of the 6cm (2⅜in) squares and hand-stitch a feather in the centre of each one with cream sewing thread, using small oversewing stitches across the spine (*fig 1*). Knot the thread on the reverse to start and finish.

fig 1

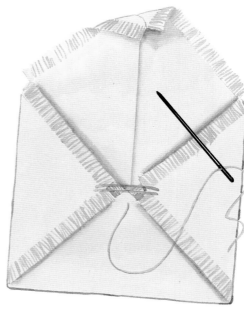

fig 4

4 Sew three wooden beads onto a further four of the 6cm (2⅜in) linen squares. Place the first bead horizontally in the centre, then add one on each side 1cm (⅜in) away. Sew through the centre of each bead about three times to secure it (*fig 2*), knotting the thread on the reverse as in step 3.

fig 2

5 Take the four 3cm (1¼in) linen squares and remove a few fabric threads all round to make frayed edges about 4mm (⅛in) deep. Place each small square diagonally onto one of the remaining 6cm (2⅜in) squares. Pin in place and sew a few stitches through the centre of both squares to hold them together. Place a stone bead over the stitches and sew in place as for the wooden beads (*fig 3*).

fig 3

6 Take the large 9cm (3½in) squares and fray the edges for 5mm (³⁄₁₆in) all around. Finger-press a diagonal fold across the squares each way to form a cross. Fold the four corners into the centre of the cross (*fig 4*) and press flat. Catch the centre points with a few small backstitches. Add a decorative pearl bead to the centre of each square and stitch in place as for the previous beads.

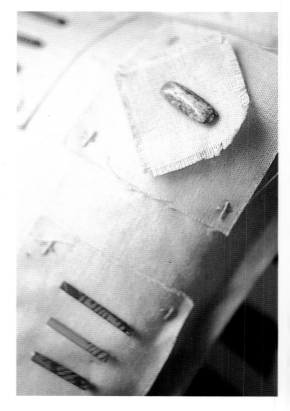

7 Referring to the photograph (right), place all the decorated squares on the cushion front, spacing them evenly. Leave a 3cm (1¼in) border all around the outer edge for the seam allowance and topstitched edging. Pin the squares in place.

8 Thread a needle with a 45cm (17¾in) length of cream buttonhole thread. Stitch a small cross stitch through the corner of one of the squares, starting and finishing the stitch on the reverse with a knot. Trim the thread. Re-knot the thread end and continue to stitch the next corner (*fig 5*). It is best not to carry any threads across on the reverse as they may pull and distort the fabric. Continue to stitch all the squares in place in this way. Remove the pins.

9 Now make up the cushion. Take the two back panels and turn under 1cm (⅜in) along one long edge of each. Press. Turn under another 1cm (⅜in) and press. Pin and stitch along the edge of the hem either by machine or by hand. Lay the two back panels on top of the completed cushion front, right sides together, overlapping the hemmed edges of the panels. Pin and baste (*fig 6*). Sew a 1cm (⅜in) seam all around the cushion cover.

10 Clip the excess fabric from the corners and turn the cushion cover right side out. Press the seams. Place the cushion pad inside and pin around the edge through the front and back of

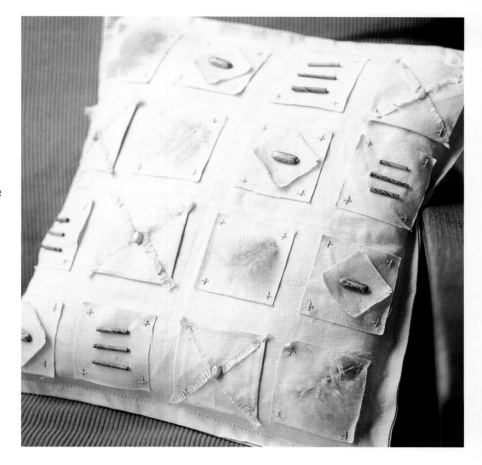

the cover so that the pad fits snugly. Remove the pad and topstitch along the pinned line, approximately 1cm (⅜in) in from the edge of the cover. Pull the thread ends through to the reverse and knot to secure. Trim any stray threads. Reinsert the cushion pad to finish.

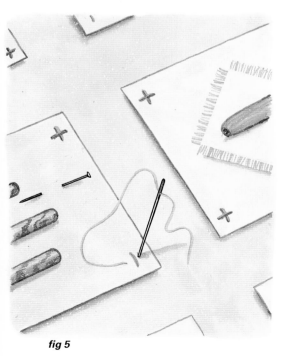

fig 5

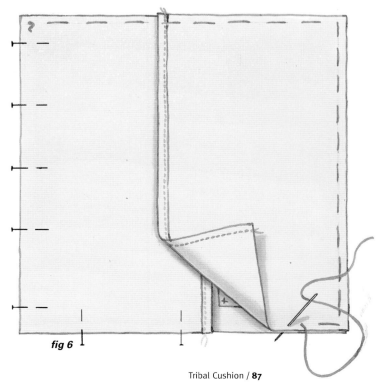

fig 6

Log Cabin Sofa Throw

The strong colours in this small quilt reflect the bright, sumptuous silks used for Indian saris. On each block, contrasting strips of shot silk are pivoted around a central gold square. Although the Log Cabin technique chosen for the project is traditional, the blocks are stitched together randomly to create a painterly effect. Stripes, diagonals and diamonds can also be created by placing the vibrant blocks in a regular pattern.

Materials and Equipment

- Shot dupion silk in the following colours: reds (wine, crimson, rose); greens (bottle, sage, lime); purples (aubergine, lavender, bluebell). You will need 50 x 114cm (20 x 45in) of each colour except aubergine, where 170 x 114cm (67 x 45in) is required
- 20 x 114cm (8 x 45in) gold shot dupion silk
- 120 x 120cm (48 x 48in) 57g (2oz) wadding
- 114 x 114cm (45 x 45in) dark blue backing fabric
- Invisible nylon machine thread
- Mid grey sewing thread
- Sewing machine
- Rotary cutter and mat
- Transparent grid ruler
- Quilters' safety pins
- Iron
- Basic sewing kit (see page 120)

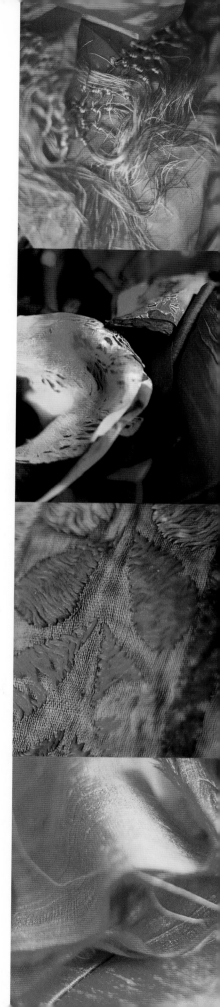

Method

1 Fold each silk piece (except gold) in half, selvedge to selvedge. Fold in half again the other way. Using the rotary cutter and mat (see page 120), cut strips 4cm (1½in) wide x the length of the silks, following the fabric grain (*fig 1*). (If you cut selvedge to selvedge, the fabric tends to fray more.) Cut four extra strips 5cm (2in) wide x the length of aubergine silk.

2 Cut the gold silk into 25 squares each measuring 4 x 4cm (1½ x 1½in). All the Log Cabin blocks are pieced around a central gold square, working from the light fabrics out towards the dark fabrics (see page 124). N.B. Seam allowances are 5mm (³⁄₁₆in) throughout.

3 Begin piecing the first block as follows. Using the mid grey thread, sew one of the centre gold squares to a light strip (e.g. rose), right sides together (*fig 2*). Reverse-stitch each end of the seam. Trim away the excess strip to make it even with the edge of the centre square. Press the seam away from the centre.

fig 1

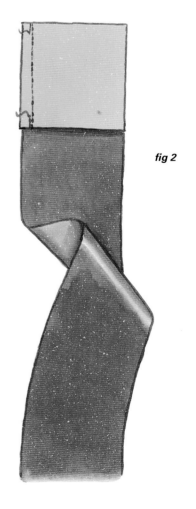

fig 2

4 Select the same light fabric (rose) for the next strip. Join to the long edge of the pieced centre, right sides together (*fig 3*), making sure that you reverse-stitch the ends of the seam. Trim away the excess strip to make the ends even with the pieced centre.

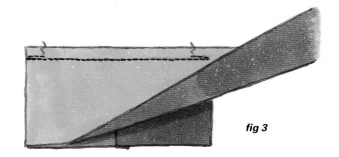

fig 3

5 Choose the light fabric from one of the other colourways (e.g. bluebell). Piece this third strip along the left-hand edge of the pieced centre, stitching and trimming as before (*fig 4*).

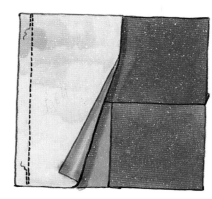

fig 4

6 Continue piecing the strips from the centre outwards as before until the first Log Cabin block is complete. Work from light to dark shades following the order shown in *fig 5*. The different colourways for the blocks are as follows (*fig 6*):
A Purples/Reds; B Reds/Greens;
C Greens/Purples; D Reds/Purples;
E Greens/Reds; F Purples/Greens.
For a quilt identical to the one shown, you will need: four of Block A; six of Block B; five of Block C; four of Block D; three of Block E; three of Block F – a total of 25 blocks.

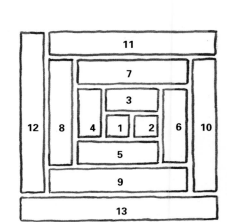

fig 5

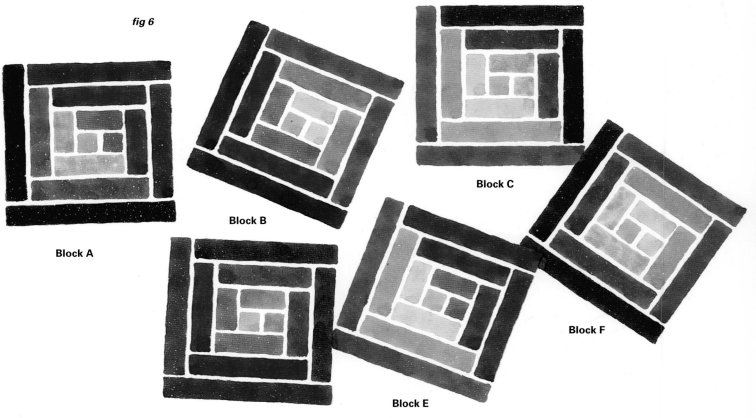

fig 6

Block A

Block B

Block C

Block D

Block E

Block F

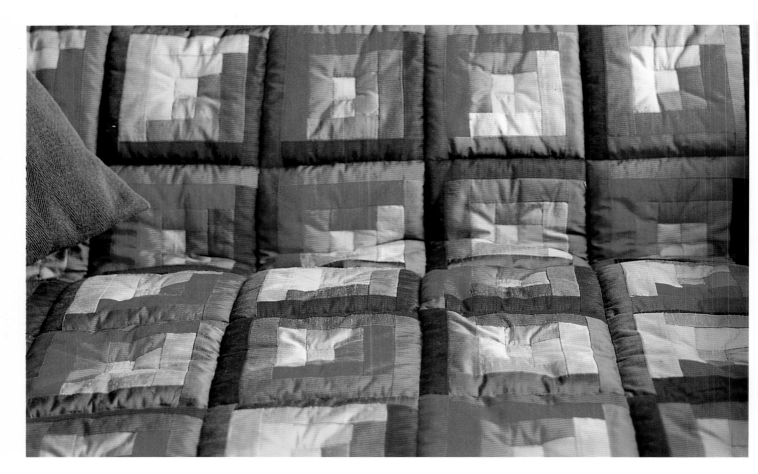

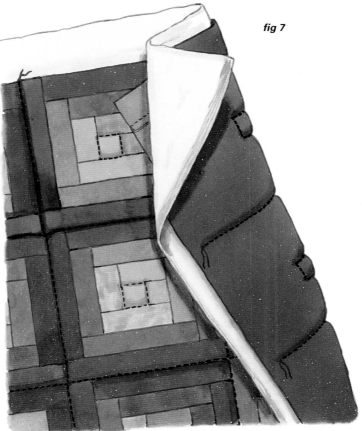

fig 7

7 Lay the blocks out on the floor in the same arrangement as on the quilt shown, or try variations of your own. Keep the gold square at the centre with the small square of equal size to its right. With right sides together and still taking a 5mm (³⁄₁₆in) seam allowance, sew the blocks together to make your chosen design. Work row by row, then sew all five rows to each other. You are now ready to quilt.

8 Make a quilt 'sandwich' by layering up the backing fabric, the wadding and the pieced top (see page 130). Hold all three layers together by pinning through them at intervals with quilters' safety pins.

9 Set the sewing machine to stitch length 4. Preferably using invisible nylon machine thread, quilt 'in the ditch' around each block (see page 131). Then quilt 'in the ditch' around each of the gold centre squares (*fig 7*). Remember either to reverse-stitch at the beginning and end of each line of stitching or bring the thread ends through to the back and knot. Trim all thread ends to finish. Trim any excess wadding and backing fabric from around the edge of the quilt.

10 For the binding, use the 5cm (2in) wide strips previously cut from the aubergine silk. Trim two to match the finished quilt length and two to match the finished width + 4cm (1½in). With right sides together, pin one shorter binding strip along one side of the quilt 5mm (³⁄₁₆in) in from the quilt edge. Stitch a seam 1.5cm (⅝in) in from the quilt edge (*fig 8*).

11 Fold the binding over to the reverse of the quilt and fold under a 1cm (³⁄₈in) turning along the remaining raw edge. Slip stitch this edge of the binding in place. Repeat with the other shorter binding strip for the opposite side of the quilt. Trim off any excess.

12 Then bind the two remaining sides of the quilt in the same way, first turning under the raw edges of the binding at the short ends to neaten them (*fig 9*).

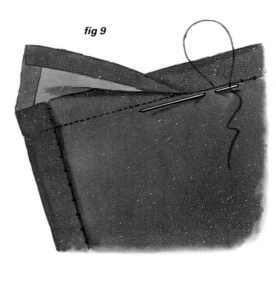

fig 9

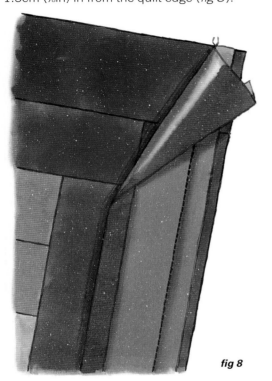

fig 8

Masai Window Covering

This striking curtain was inspired by a Masai feather headdress made up of rows of iridescent turquoise feathers interspersed with clusters of scarlet feathers. The repeating patterns of the headdress are echoed in the curtain by the colourful bands of strip piecing sewn at intervals onto a backing of translucent blue voile. The curtain can be adapted to fit any window simply by changing the size of the voile backing and the bands to fit.

Materials and Equipment

- 2m (2⅛yd) blue voile 150cm (59in) wide (or to fit chosen window)
- 'Fat quarters' (see page 142) of marbled effect cotton fabric in the following colours: cerise, pink, scarlet, orange, peach, yellow, dark blue, turquoise, purple, deep lavender
- 'Fat quarters' of plain cotton fabric in sky blue and lilac
- Anchor machine embroidery thread: 3 reels of navy 2548
- Sewing thread in red and blue
- Sewing machine
- Rotary cutter and mat
- Transparent grid ruler
- Quilters' safety pins
- Iron
- Basic sewing kit (see page 120)

Method

1 Trim a 40cm (16in) strip off the length of blue voile. Cut this into 17 small strips measuring 10 x 20cm (4 x 8in) and place to one side. These will form the tabs along the top of the curtain.

2 The striped panels are constructed with strip piecing. The fabric is cut into strips of random widths, which are then joined at different angles. For this project, you will need to make two blue panels and four pink/orange panels.

3 To make the blue panels, cut strips from the blue range of fat quarters using the rotary cutter, ruler and mat (see page 120) (*fig 1*). The strips should measure 28cm (11in) long and be of random widths.

4 Set up the sewing machine for straight stitch and thread it with blue sewing thread. Begin to join the blue strips together at different angles to create a pattern of irregular stripes (*fig 2*). Continue to join strips until you have made a 160cm (63in) length. Trim the irregular seam allowances to 6mm (¼in). Repeat to make the second blue panel. Using the rotary cutter, mat and ruler, trim the completed panels to 25cm (10in) wide.

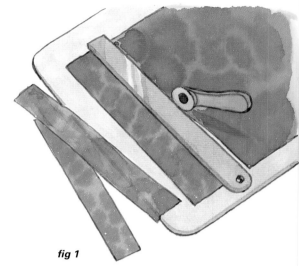

fig 1

5 To make the pink/orange panels, cut the appropriate fat quarters of fabric into strips of random width and 30cm (12in) long. Using red sewing thread in the machine, join them as for the blue strips until you have made a 160cm (63in) length. Trim the irregular seam allowances and edges as before. Using the rotary cutter, mat and ruler, cut the pink/orange strip into four panels of equal width (*fig 3*).

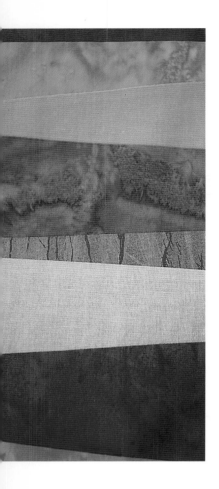

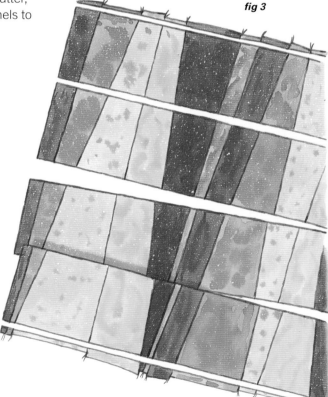

fig 3

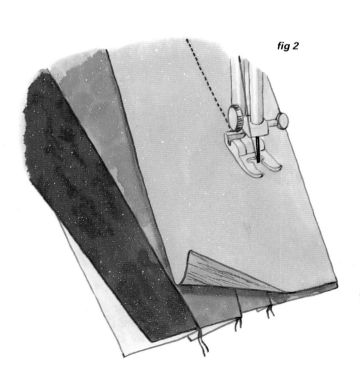

fig 2

6 Thread the machine with navy machine embroidery thread. Turn under a double 5mm (³⁄₁₆in) hem on each long side of the blue voile and pin. Stitch close to the turned hem edge and press (*fig 4*).

7 Lay the voile on a flat surface with the finished hems at the back. Lay the strip-pieced panels on top, right side up, arranging them at regular intervals across the fabric or as you wish. Pin, baste, then machine stitch them in place.

8 To finish the raw edges of the strip-pieced panels, set the machine to zigzag stitch with a width of 5 and a length of 0.5. Test the stitching on a scrap of fabric first to check that you are achieving a smooth satin stitch. N.B. It may help to loosen the top thread tension slightly. Work satin stitch along all the raw edges of the panels (*fig 5*).

9 Turn up the lower edge of the curtain by 2cm (¾in) and press. Turn up a further 5cm (2in), then press, pin and stitch the hem in place. Turn down the top edge of the curtain by 1cm (⅜in) and press. Fold down another 2cm (¾in), then press, pin and baste.

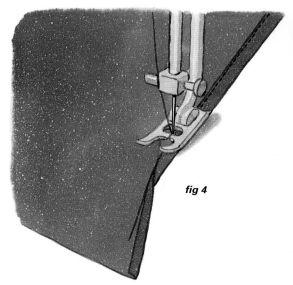

fig 4

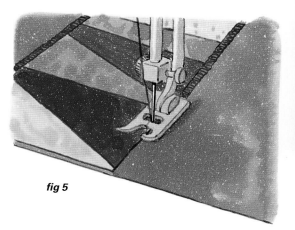

fig 5

fig 6

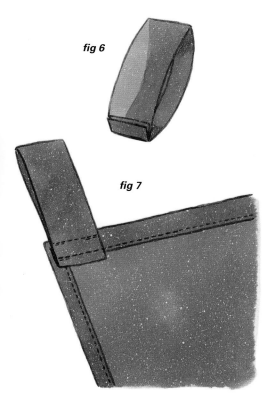

fig 7

10 Take the 17 strips of blue voile to make the tab tops. With right sides together, fold each one in half lengthways and stitch along the long edge, taking a 1cm (⅜in) seam allowance. Turn to the right side and press flat with the seam centred to the back. Fold in half, then turn the raw edges up by 1cm (⅜in) and press (*fig 6*).

11 With wrong sides together, pin and baste the tabs evenly along the top of the curtain over the folded hem edge (*fig 7*). Catch the tabs in place with two rows of machine stitching, positioning one row close to the outer edge of the curtain and the other row close to the folded hem edge. Reverse stitch at each end of the seams to secure them. Finally, remove the basting stitches and press the curtain.

food

Above: *Pineapple leaves and skin make strong repeating patterns for strip or block piecing.*
Opposite page: top left – *Cut triangular wedges and piece them together to recreate the cut section of a luscious orange. Appliqué as a motif on to a background fabric;*
top right – *Shimmering organza stitched in bands and blocks is suggested by this picture of herb ice cubes;*
below left – *A variety of shapes can be drawn from a table setting such as this. Look for ovals, concentric circles, triangles and wedges;*
below right – *This melon with its detailed centre of tiny seeds would lend itself to interpretation in quilting.*

Exotic or plain, food is an essential part of our everyday lives. Whether from a hypermarket, a fruit and vegetable stall or harvested fresh, it has visual appeal that designers can exploit in many ways.

Food may be a somewhat surprising source of inspiration for patchwork and quilting designs, but it is something we all have access to and is diverse in shape, colour, texture and presentation. Rows of tins and boxes in packaging designed to catch the eye do not need to be developed much further into a design for piecing or quilting. The images and lettering can be abstracted into stripes and other geometric shapes which can then be developed into blocks with interesting proportions. Simply lay a sheet of tracing paper over the labels and square off each area. Match your fabrics to the colours of the packaging. If you can visit a local market, take photographs of the stacked boxes of fruit and vegetables or the displays of fresh fish and seafood. Their colours and textures will suggest numerous ideas for fabric shades and piecing patterns. For a close-up view, slice a fruit or vegetable to get a cross-section. Sketch the shapes on graph paper, then repeat and overlap them for an all-over quilting design or simplify them for a pieced or appliqué border. Don't ignore the contents of your own store cupboard for ideas. Grains or nuts in a bowl or jar give interesting patterns to develop into closely worked lines of quilting. Small and large pasta shapes scattered at random onto a bright cloth will give yet more ideas. This section will show you just how versatile food images can be.

Right – *Skewered foods on a plate show simple blocks of contrasting colours laid in lines. Strip piecing such as Seminole patchwork could be developed from this image.*
Below – *Biscuit colours and shiny metallics provide a sophisticated yet sumptuous palette, especially if worked in velvets and satins.*

Opposite page: top – *Pots containing herbs provide a fresh colour scheme for a patchwork project. The shapes suggest a burnt edge frill suitable for a cushion border;*
below left – *The concentric rings of hexagons which form English patchwork could be derived from this stylized image;*
below right – *This photograph suggests Cathedral Window blocks in pastel silks with tiny beads sewn over the corner joins.*

Left – *Create a classic pattern for a quilted border or a centre medallion from a plate of strawberries.*

Right – *The soft blended colours on this papaya look like hand-dyed fabric which could be used to personalize any project.*

Opposite page – *Slices of beautiful ruby-coloured grapefruits would make a strong design for a tablecloth with a minimalist feel, using curved blocks in amongst plain ones.*

Left – *Figs offer wonderful imagery and a rich, dark palette. Quilt, appliqué or piece the shapes to make a luxurious curtain tie-back in velvet and silk.*

Left – *Succulent slices of watermelon are interesting images. The shape, texture and colour contrast make a simple yet stylish abstract design.*

Right – *Clusters of redcurrants suggest spirals quilted closely together to form an overall background texture.*

Zest Napkins

Crisp, fresh and summery, these napkins are just right for a sophisticated picnic or a table set with bright crockery and vases of flowers. The orange slices are translated into simple appliqué motifs and the whole effect is diffused by a layer of organdie to prevent the colour contrast being too stark. This technique is a form of shadow quilting.

Materials and Equipment
(for two napkins)
- 80 x 40cm (31½ x 15¾in) white cotton voile
- 80 x 40cm (31½ x 15¾in) white cotton organdie
- 20 x 30cm (8 x 11¾in) pale yellow cotton fabric
- 20 x 30cm (8 x 11¾in) orange cotton fabric
- 20 x 60cm (8 x 23½in) fusible fabric bond
- 2.5m (2¾yd) lemon satin bias binding, 2cm (¾in) wide
- Cream sewing thread
- Anchor machine embroidery thread: one reel in yellow 2110
- Sewing machine
- Rotary cutter and mat
- Transparent grid ruler
- Quilters' safety pins
- Sharp coloured pencil or fabric marker
- Iron
- Embroidery hoop
- Basic sewing kit (see page 120)

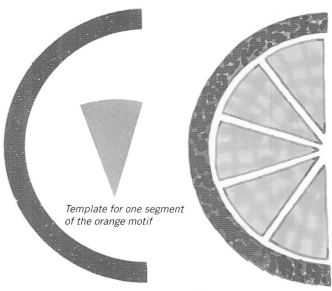

*Template for one segment
of the orange motif*

Template for the semicircular orange rind

Placement guide for half orange slice

Placement guide for whole orange slice

Method

1 Using the rotary cutter, mat and ruler, cut two squares from the cotton voile each measuring 40 x 40cm (15¾ x 15¾in). Repeat for the organdie, but lay these aside. With a sharp coloured pencil or fabric marker, mark a 30cm (11¾in) square centrally on each piece of voile to show the outer edge of the napkins.

2 Cut two pieces of fusible fabric bond each measuring 20 x 30cm (8 x 11¾in). Onto the paper side of one piece trace off 50 triangular segments (see template above), as well as two strips 1cm (⅜in) wide x 30cm (11¾in) long. Iron the fusible fabric bond onto the back of the yellow fabric. On the other piece of fusible fabric bond, trace off ten semicircles for the rind (see template above), and two strips 1cm (⅜in) wide x 30cm (11¾in) long. Iron this piece onto the back of the orange fabric (*fig 1*). Trim around all the motifs and peel off the paper backing.

3 Arrange three half slices of orange on one square of voile (see placement guide above), 1cm (⅜in) up from the lower marked edge. Place a yellow and an orange strip above them. Then arrange a whole orange slice 2cm (¾in) in from the marked top and side edges. Iron the motifs in place.

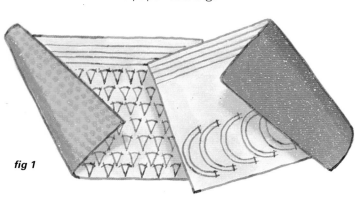

fig 1

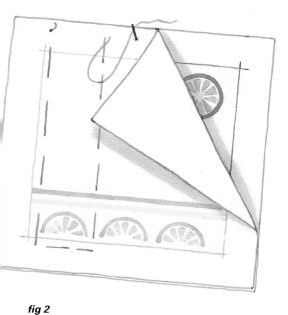

fig 2

4 Lay the organdie on top of the bonded fabric and pin in place. Using the cream sewing thread, baste a grid of stitches through both layers to hold them together for quilting (*fig 2*).

5 Set up the sewing machine for free embroidery (see page 134). Place the napkin in a hoop, ensuring that the fabric is stretched taut. Using the yellow machine embroidery thread and an embroidery foot, stitch around all the orange segments individually, then stitch around the rinds (*fig 3*). Reset the machine for straight stitching and stitch along each edge of the two strips. Repeat steps 3, 4 and 5 for the second napkin.

6 Take out the basting stitches and lightly press the napkins on the reverse. Trim them around the marked lines so that they measure 30cm (11¾in) square.

7 Cut the bias binding into two equal lengths. With right sides together, pin the binding in place around each napkin, matching raw edges. At each corner, fold it at a 45° angle and crease it (*fig 4a*). Machine stitch up to the crease, using the yellow machine embroidery thread (*fig 4b*). Fold the mitred corner as shown and stitch along the second side (*fig 4c*). Turn the binding over to the reverse (*fig 4d*) and pin. Fold the corners into mitres. Slip stitch the edge of the binding and the corner seams in place (*fig 4e*). Press to finish.

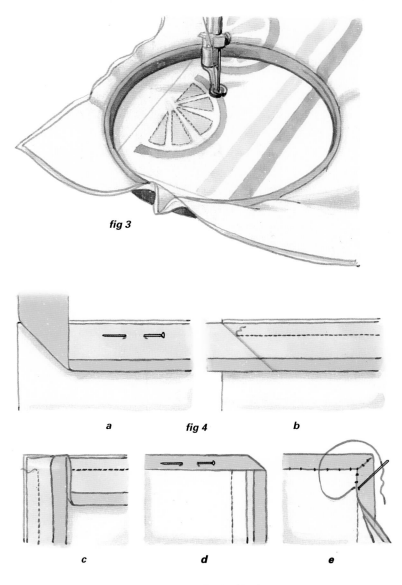

fig 3

a   **fig 4**   *b*

c   *d*   *e*

Slashed Patchwork Throw

The colours of this throw were inspired by fruits and edible flowers. The diagonal slashing lines represent the finely sliced fruits lying prepared on a chopping board. An interesting feature of this quilt is that it actually makes use of all those tiny bits and pieces of fabric and thread left over from other projects.

Materials and Equipment
- 36 x 114cm (14 x 45in) dupion silk in each of lilac, gold, orange and pale green
- 114 x 114cm (45 x 45in) wine cotton backing fabric
- 100 x 140cm (40 x 55in) wine rayon velvet
- Shredded fabric and thread waste (approximately 36 handfuls)
- Anchor machine embroidery thread: one reel in each of lilac 2463, gold 2110, orange 2285, green 2753
- Sewing machine
- Rotary cutter and mat (optional)
- Transparent grid ruler (optional)
- Iron
- Basic sewing kit (see page 120)

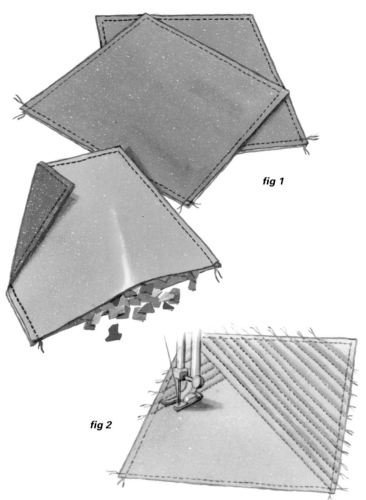

fig 1

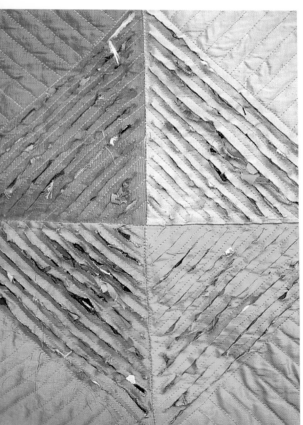

fig 2

Method

1 Using a rotary cutter, mat and ruler (see page 120) or scissors, cut out nine squares measuring 18 x 18cm (7 x 7in) from each of the pieces of silk fabric. Cut out 36 squares measuring 18 x 18cm (7 x 7in) from the wine cotton backing fabric. Lay the silk squares on top of the backing squares with the silk right side up. Pin the silk and backing squares together and edge stitch around three sides 4mm (⅛in) from the edge to form a 'pocket'.

2 Fill each pocket with a generous handful of shredded fabric and thread waste and spread out evenly. Edge stitch along the fourth side of the pockets to close them (*fig 1*). Press gently with an iron to flatten.

3 Choose a matching embroidery thread and machine stitch a diagonal line across one of the square pockets. On one half of the square, echo the diagonal line by stitching lines parallel to it and about 1cm (⅜in) apart. On the remaining half, stitch lines at right angles to the diagonal line, again placing them about 1cm (⅜in) apart. Repeat for all the squares. They should now look slightly quilted (*fig 2*).

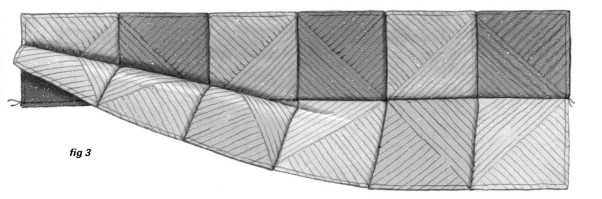

fig 3

4 Using the detail photograph on the previous page as a guide, join the squares together in rows, taking a 1.5cm (⅝in) seam allowance. As you work across each row, make sure the quilting lines that echo the initial diagonal line meet to form diamonds (*fig 3*).

5 Using small, sharp scissors, cut along the centre of the stitched channels that form each diamond (*fig 4*). Shake to loosen any fabric or thread scraps that have not been caught by the stitched lines.

6 Trim the velvet fabric to a square measuring approximately 92 x 92cm (36¼ x 36¼in) or to fit the quilted panel. Lay the quilted panel on top of the velvet, wrong sides together, and pin. Stitch around the raw edge to hold the layers in place.

7 From the remaining velvet, cut two strips each 7.5 x 92cm (3 x 36¼in) and two strips 7.5 x 95cm (3 x 37½in). With right sides together, pin the two shorter binding strips to opposite sides of the quilt, with the binding 1cm (⅜in) in from the quilted edge. Sew in place, taking a 1cm (⅜in) seam allowance (*fig 5*). Fold the remaining binding to the back of the quilt, turn the raw edges under and slip stitch in place.

8 Apply the two longer binding strips to the remaining sides of the quilt in the same way, first folding the short raw edges under by 1.5cm (⅝in) to prevent them fraying (*fig 6*).

fig 4

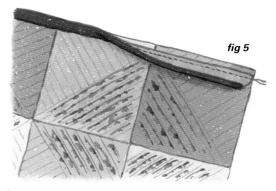

fig 5

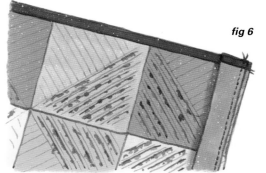

fig 6

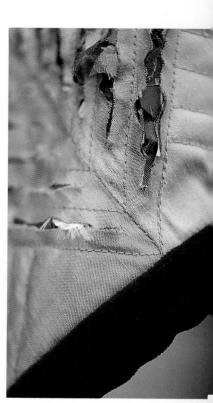

Openwork Bed Drape

Rows of beautifully packaged foodstuffs stacked close together in a delicatessen suggested simple patchworked squares. Labels often add an extra decorative detail to packets – this has been recreated here by appliquéing gold motifs onto the squares. The unique openwork effect is achieved by patching the squares together using water soluble fabric.

Materials and Equipment
- 75 x 114cm (29½ x 45in) midnight blue organdie
- 75 x 114cm (29½ x 45in) dark petrol organdie
- 30 x 114cm (11¾ x 45in) gold/pink shot organdie
- 30 x 114cm (11¾ x 45in) metallic tissue in gold
- 30 x 114cm (11¾ x 45in) fusible fabric bond
- 3m (3¼yd) cold water soluble fabric, 150cm (59in) wide
- 7m (7½yd) navy satin bias binding, 2cm (¾in) wide
- Anchor machine embroidery thread: six reels in Cristalle metallic gold
- Sewing machine
- Rotary cutter and mat
- Transparent grid ruler
- Two tubes of Fray Check or PVA glue
- Small paintbrush
- Iron
- Basic sewing kit (see page 120)

Templates for the gold appliqué shapes

Templates for the gold appliqué shapes

Template A

Template B

Template C

Template D

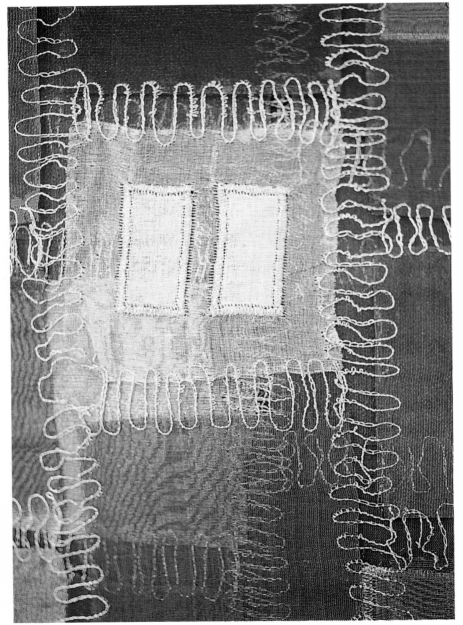

Method

1 Using the rotary cutter, ruler and mat (see page 120), cut the three pieces of organdie fabric into 7.5cm (3in) squares. You will need 408 squares in total. Using the small paintbrush, brush Fray Check or PVA glue carefully around the raw edges to prevent the fabric from fraying (*fig 1*). Leave to dry.

2 Cut the water soluble fabric into strips 8.5cm (3⅜in) wide by 3m (3¼yd) long. From these, cut 17 strips 70cm (27½in) in length ready for assembling the organdie squares in step 4.

fig 1

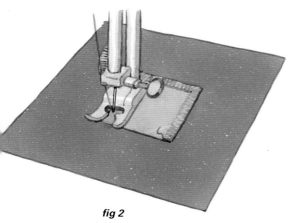

fig 2

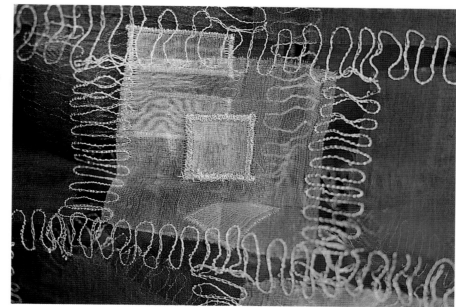

3 Trace off the templates for the appliqué shapes (opposite) onto the paper side of the fusible fabric bond. You will need 22 of each motif. Iron the fusible fabric bond onto the back of the metallic gold tissue. Trim around the shapes, then peel off the paper backing. Lay the shapes onto 88 of the organdie squares (approximately 35 in midnight blue, 35 in dark petrol and 18 in gold/pink). Iron the shapes in place. Set up the sewing machine for satin stitch. Using the metallic gold thread, work satin stitch around each motif (*fig 2*).

4 Take a 70cm (27½in) strip of cold water soluble fabric and pin 24 organdie squares along it in a random colourway, interspersing appliquéd squares among plain ones. Follow the pinning method shown in *fig 3* as it is very economical with the fabric. Leave a gap of about 1cm (⅜in) between each square. N.B. If the cold water soluble fabric tears during use, simply overlay another piece to patch. All layers will eventually be dissolved.

5 Set up the sewing machine for free embroidery (see page 134) and thread it with metallic gold thread. Loosen the top thread tension slightly as metallic thread has a tendency to snap more easily than ordinary machine embroidery thread. You should not need an embroidery hoop for this process as the water soluble fabric is fairly stiff. Stitch across the gap between the first two squares in a 'serpentine' fashion in order to catch the edge of each square as you move along (*fig 4*). Keep the stitches small. Repeat until all the squares are stitched together, then trim any thread ends.

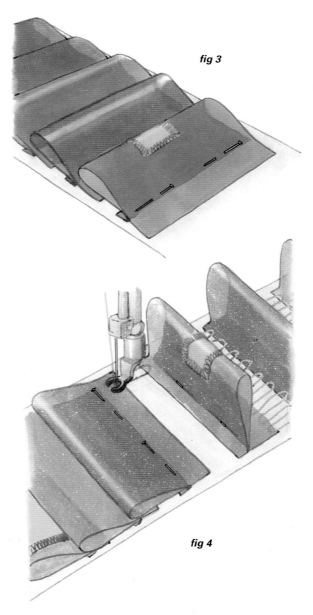

fig 3

fig 4

▶

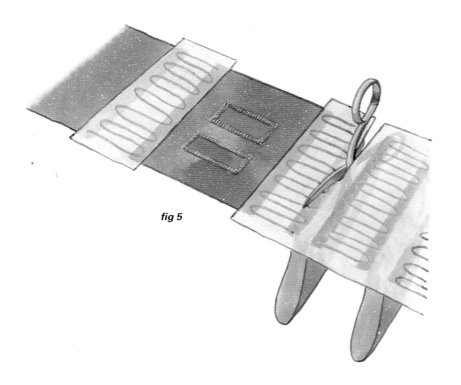

fig 5

6 Repeat steps 4 and 5 until you have 17 strips of 24 squares. It is best to remove the cold water soluble fabric stage by stage. First, trim away the unstitched water soluble fabric from underneath the organdie squares (*fig 5*).

7 You will now have strips about 205cm (81in) long. Join the strips in sections of no more than four as follows. Pin a length of the water soluble fabric between two of the strips, keeping them 1cm (⅜in) apart. It is important to offset the strips so that the squares form a half drop pattern, otherwise the fabric becomes too flimsy (*fig 6*). Work serpentine stitch between the strips as before. Add on two more strips in the same way.

fig 6

8 When you have joined four strips together, dissolve the cold water soluble fabric. Fill a washing-up bowl with cold water and place one or two folded towels beside it. Pull the strips through the water, agitating them slightly to dissolve the water soluble fabric (*fig 7*). N.B. The more often you wash water soluble fabric, the softer it becomes, so if it does not dissolve first time, dip the strips in the water again. Place the strips on the towels to absorb the excess liquid. The organdie may warp at this stage. Do not panic! Press it back into shape whilst damp, using a steam iron and cloths to protect the ironing surface and iron.

9 Repeat this process until all the strips have been joined in groups and washed. Join the groups together, then wash out the final strips of water soluble fabric. Press the organdie again. Trim the uneven edges at the top and bottom of the drape. It should now measure approximately 124 x 205cm (48½ x 81in).

10 To finish the drape, it can either be laid onto a silk backing or left transparent. Bind the raw edges with satin bias binding (*fig 8*), as for the Zest Napkins on page 107.

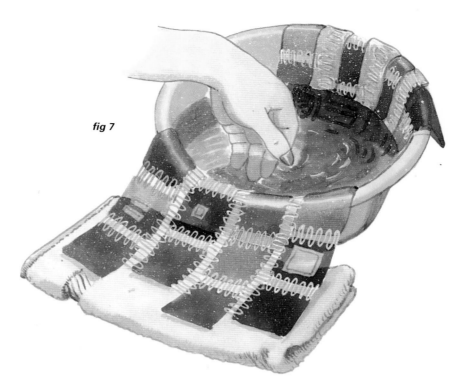

fig 7

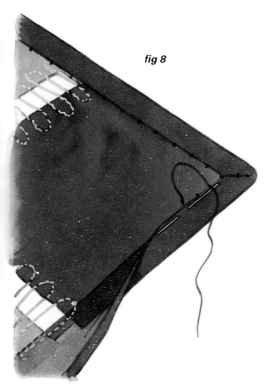

fig 8

techniques, materials and equipment

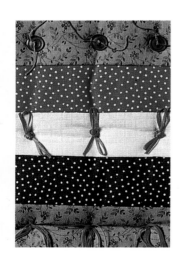

Above: *Knotted and tied quilting, page 132.*
Opposite page: above left – *English patchwork, page 127;* **above right** – *Machine quilting, page 130;* **below left** – *Hand quilting, page 131;* **below right** – *Crazy patchwork, page 129.*

The sheer variety of products available on the market nowadays can be overwhelming. This chapter breaks down some of the most used and quoted techniques, materials and equipment in patchwork and quilting and, hopefully, simplifies them.

It should not be necessary to rush out and buy lots of specialized equipment to begin the projects in this book as much of the equipment required can be found in most domestic sewing boxes. As your interest in patchwork grows, it is a good idea to look out for specialist fairs that demonstrate and sell fabric and equipment. You can usually pick up more unusual products and fabrics from these outlets, and often at discounted rates. Large items such as sewing machines should be thoroughly experimented with before you buy – most retailers are quite happy to let you try them out in the shop first.

All the techniques used in the book are featured individually in this chapter, with simple examples demonstrating clearly how each basic technique should look. Refer to this section first and try it out before proceeding with a project, particularly if you are new to a method of working. Practice does make perfect and it will help build confidence. You will not find every technique easy to master, as people are naturally more responsive to some working methods than others. Take things slowly, prepare well and have all materials to hand before you try.

Essential Equipment

Some of the equipment listed below may already be part of your household sewing box, but it is worth investing a little more in certain items to ensure that they are of the best quality.

SCISSORS

Dressmaking scissors: a good quality pair will last for years as they can be re-sharpened. They are available in different sizes and it is a good idea to try them out before you buy in order to find a pair that feels right. Never use fabric scissors on paper and take care not to blunt them by accidentally cutting over pins.

Small, sharp-pointed embroidery scissors: these are useful for trimming threads after sewing a seam or working some embroidery. They are also easier to manage than large scissors when cutting out small motifs and trimming layers of fabric.

Paper scissors: use any handy household scissors that are fairly sharp. Useful for cutting out patchwork templates and paper patterns for motifs.

NEEDLES

Embroidery needles: sharp pointed needles in a variety of sizes with a slightly larger eye than standard hand-sewing needles.

Hand-sewing needles: these are available in a variety of sizes and are used for sewing seams and basting fabrics together.

SEWING MACHINE

A good domestic sewing machine usually performs a variety of functions. Most modern machines have a facility to convert to free machine embroidery, or the darning plate can be used. Try a variety of techniques on your machine before you buy.

TAPE MEASURE

A cloth tape measure provides accurate sizes for projects and templates and is more useful than a wind-up metal one for use with textiles.

IRON

A steam iron gives a crisp finish to patchwork projects, but never press hard on finished projects as this flattens the effect. It is best not to iron quilted items as the wadding will become compressed. Use a dry iron for bonding small shapes to a background fabric when working appliqué designs.

PINS

Pins are essential for holding the different fabrics together in patchwork and appliqué. Use glass-headed pins so that you can easily re-locate them when using them in projects.

ROTARY CUTTER

This type of cutter has a circular blade set into a plastic handle. It is useful for cutting straight lines and geometric shapes in fabric. A rotary cutter is best used in conjunction with a cutting mat.

CUTTING MAT

A soft plastic mat of variable size, useful for protecting surfaces against the blade of a rotary cutter. The surface is often self-healing, which prevents score marks appearing on it. Many cutting mats have metric and imperial grid markings on them to help make your measuring easier as you work. It is also possible to buy a mat with one side designated for cutting and the other side suitable for pressing and ironing fabric.

TRANSPARENT RULE/ OMNIGRID

A clear rectangular or triangular ruler that comes in various sizes and is ideal for patchwork projects as it usually has basic template guidelines and measurements marked on it. Use this type of ruler with the rotary cutter and cutting mat.

QUILTERS' SAFETY PINS

Large, wide safety pins suitable for pinning through different layers of wadding and fabric to secure them ready for quilting. They can be used instead of basting stitches, which may catch on the machine foot as you quilt.

HOOPS

Embroidery hoop: a wooden or plastic hoop, available in various sizes, that keeps the fabric taut for correct tension during embroidery by hand or machine.

Quilting hoop: a wide wooden hoop that can be used to hold layers of fabric and wadding in place while hand-quilting.

Transferring Designs

There are a variety of ways of transferring template shapes and quilting designs onto fabric. Some of the projects have recommended methods although other options are available.

Tracing Directly onto Fabric

This is possible where the fabric you are using is transparent or light in colour (e.g. chiffon and voile). Simply lay the fabric on top of the template or motif, secure with masking tape, and trace using a pencil, water/air soluble fabric pen or tailors' chalk. Note that pencil lines will often not wash out so the project stitching has to cover it. With the water/air soluble fabric pen, some fabrics permanently stain although I've not come across this problem. The disadvantage in using tailors' chalk is that it rubs off easily and may disappear before the design is complete.

If you wish to trace onto the reverse of the fabric, note that this method will reverse the image. To avoid this you need to reverse the tracing paper and draw over the template lines before following the above method.

Tracing and Basting

This is a good method for marking embroidery designs onto dark or difficult to mark fabric such as velvet. Trace the design onto tissue paper or tracing paper and pin it to the fabric. Stitch the design outline by hand or machine before carefully tearing away the tissue or tracing paper, leaving the stitches as a guide.

Light Box Tracing

This allows you to trace directly onto darker fabrics. Use masking tape to anchor the template or pattern to the light box then tape the fabric on top, right side up. Make sure the fabric is taut in order for it to be drawn upon. You can use pencil, water/air soluble fabric pen or tailors' chalk.

If you do not have access to a light box, tape the template and fabric to a brightly sunlit window, or make a simple light box by placing a table lamp under a glass-topped coffee table. Alternatively, the glass from a picture frame positioned over a lamp would do – but be careful with this method.

Iron-on Transfers

Transfer pencils are available in craft shops and fabric shops and will give a permanent line on fabric. Begin by tracing the design onto tracing paper with an ordinary pencil. Then reverse the paper and carefully draw over the template lines using the transfer pencil. Now place the tracing (with the transfer pencil lines facing downwards) onto the right side of the fabric and press with a warm iron. Remove the paper to leave the tracing lines on the fabric.

Fusible Fabric Bond

An easy method of transferring designs for appliqué is to use fusible fabric bond. This is a thin glue that forms a web which can be ironed between two layers of fabric to stick them together. It has a layer of waxed paper behind it in order to prevent it from sticking to the iron. Fabric bond is transparent and motifs can be traced through directly onto the paper backing before ironing onto fabric and trimming around a drawn motif. Peel the paper backing off before ironing the motif onto the background fabric.

Dressmakers' Carbon Paper

This is available in several colours to suit light or dark fabrics. Place it face down on the right side of the fabric with your pattern on top. Trace over the design lines with a hard lead pencil or a tracing wheel.

Blunt Needle or Silverpoint

This method is best used with solid-coloured fabric. Stretch the fabric on a frame, then mark around your template with the blunt needle or silverpoint (a pencil-shaped metal implement). The motif will appear as an indented line on the fabric.

Enlarging and Reducing Designs

There may be occasions when you wish to enlarge or reduce a template or motif to adapt a design to your own requirements. The quickest and easiest way to do this is by using a photocopier. A good copying shop will help you with the calculations you need to do in order to achieve the correct dimensions for your project. Then you can simply trace and transfer the template at its new size.

Making Templates

For standard popular patchwork shapes such as hexagons, you can buy different types of templates made of metal or plastic. However, some projects require special templates that you will have to make yourself.

Template Plastic

This is basically a thick sheet of transparent acetate specifically designed for making patchwork templates. When you lay it over a design drawn on graph paper, you can easily trace the shapes off and cut them out to use as templates.

Card Templates

Another method of making templates requires graph paper, thick card and spray glue. Mark out all the template shapes accurately on graph paper, adding the seam allowances if appropriate (a). Spray the reverse of the graph paper with the glue and stick it onto the thick card. Using a metal ruler and a craft knife with a cutting mat, score along the outer lines marked on the graph paper. Continue to score each line until you have cut right through the card (b). Repeat until all shapes have been cut out. Remember that it is better to work slowly and score down through the card lightly than try to press too hard and cut through in one move, since this is more likely to break the blade or cause the knife to slip.

Marking the Fabric

When you have cut out the templates by either method, lay them onto the reverse of your chosen fabric and mark around each one accurately, using tailors' chalk or a specialist marker that will either fade or wash away (c). Alternatively, a lead pencil can be used with care, as can a quilters' pencil.

Seam Allowances on Templates

Every stitcher will develop a favourite way of piecing, whether by hand or machine, and every tutor will have their own thoughts on how and where seam allowances should be added to the patches. A general rule for seam allowances is as follows.

For machine piecing, add a 6mm (¼in) seam allowance onto your card or plastic templates. This is because the machine foot acts as a guide when you are piecing, eliminating the need for a seam allowance to be marked onto the fabric.

For hand piecing, the traditional method is to cut the templates to the exact finished size of the patch. Mark around the templates on the fabric and then mark a seam allowance of 6mm (¼in) all round before cutting out. The original marked lines act as a stitching guide when seaming the patches together.

Alternatively, you can cut out the templates including the seam allowance and mark around them on the fabric. Then draw the seamline 6mm (¼in) inside the first marked lines as a stitching guide.

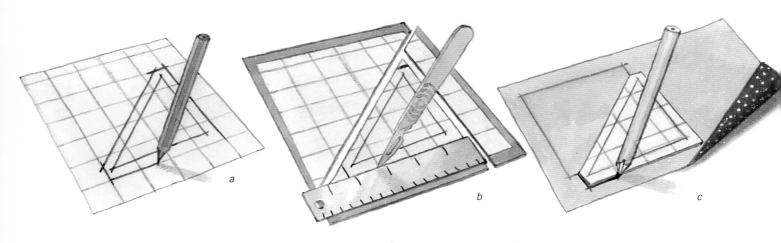

a   b   c

Patchwork Techniques

There are numerous different patchwork techniques, each with its own history, but any form of joining fabric pieces together is simple patchwork. Bear in mind that, with patchwork, some of the rules are definitely there for the breaking.

Strip Patchwork

Strip or string patchwork is a very simple form of patchwork that is ideal for using up random widths of fabric in order to create a new fabric.

Cut strips of varying widths from a variety of patterned and plain fabrics. It is best to keep to the same weight of fabric for this technique, i.e. all cottons or all silks, as the finished effect may otherwise look rather uneven.

Join the strips together by hand or machine using a straight stitch and taking a seam allowance of 6mm (¼in). Sew the strips in parallel widths or join them at angles for a more dramatic effect. The strip pieced fabric can then be used in other projects as an appliqué section, an all-over design or a border.

Seminole Patchwork

Seminole patchwork owes its origins to the Seminole Indians in North America. It is ideal for borders or for insertions in a garment. It is best to machine piece Seminole patchwork as this is much quicker than sewing by hand.

Cut strips of fabric crossways (selvedge to selvedge) from a variety of coloured cottons. The strips can be of even or random widths, but they must be of equal length. Sew the strips together, taking a 6mm (¼in) seam allowance.

Once all strips are joined, press the seams to one side (a). Use a transparent ruler and fabric marker to draw parallel lines across the pieced fabric. Cut new strips using a rotary cutter or scissors (b). Join these short sections together, but offset them slightly, e.g. by one fabric strip down or according to your chosen design. You can set them at an angle if you wish (c). Once all strips have been joined, press lightly and trim the top and lower edges to straighten them (d).

If the Seminole panel is to be inserted into a larger item, it is helpful to make the two outer strips wider by 6mm (¼in) in the first instance to allow for joining them to a border.

a

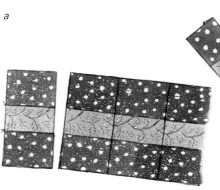

b

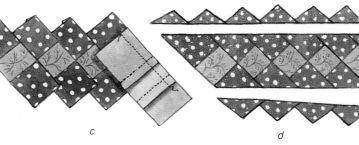

c

d

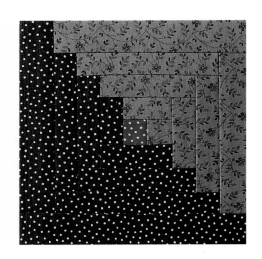

Basic Log Cabin

This effective pattern is named after the American pioneers' tradition of building houses from logs, but dates back further than was originally thought. It is based on strip piecing and can be pieced onto a foundation fabric if preferred.

Usually worked around a centre square, one half of the block consists of light-coloured fabrics and the other half of dark-coloured fabrics. Begin by cutting strips approximately 4 x 25cm (1½ x 10in) in your chosen colours. Cut a square 4 x 4cm (1½ x 1½in) for the centre of the block.

With right sides together, begin by sewing a light strip to the centre square, taking a 6mm (¼in) seam allowance. Reverse stitch the seam ends to secure (a). Trim away the excess strip to make it even with the centre square. Press all seam allowances away from the centre.

Select the same light fabric for the next strip. Join to the new centre with right sides facing (b) and trim away the excess as before. Choose a dark fabric and join along the left edge of the pieced centre (c).

Continue to join all strips in the same way, rotating the block as you go and ensuring that the light fabrics are placed to one side and the dark fabrics to the other.

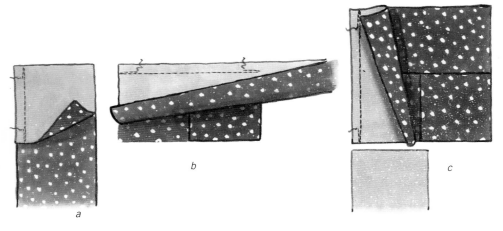

a

b

c

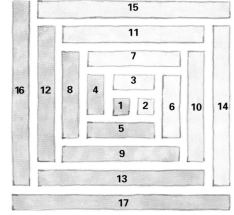

Courthouse Steps

This simple variation of Log Cabin patchwork involves adding the dark and light strips to opposite sides of the centre square. It plays even more on tonal contrast than basic Log Cabin patchwork. Piecing Courthouse Steps blocks together can make for a striking, bold geometric design. Try using shiny fabrics in some blocks and matt fabrics in others for a subtle play of light throughout the design.

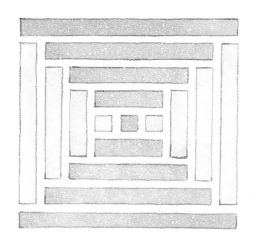

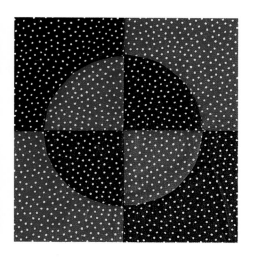

Basic Curved Block

The basic curved block shown consists of four quarters, each made up of two shapes with curved edges. There are many variations on curved blocks and, as with all patchwork techniques, clever effects can be created by the way the different fabrics are combined.

It is best to plot templates on graph paper, using a pair of compasses to draw the curves. All curved edges should follow the bias of the cloth, while the straight edges should lie on the straight grain (a). Depending on your method of construction, either add the seam allowance to the template or to the fabric (see page 122). Mark notches on the curved edges.

When joining two curved edges together, the curves bend in opposite directions, so you will need to ease the seam allowances as you pin (b). Sew the patches together with small stitches and press the seams to one side. Join the first two quarters of the block as shown (c). Join the other two quarters, then make up the whole block (d)

a

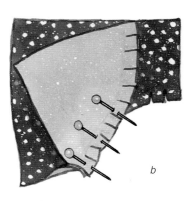

b

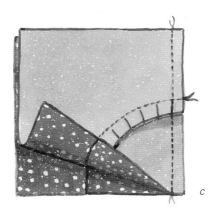

c

d

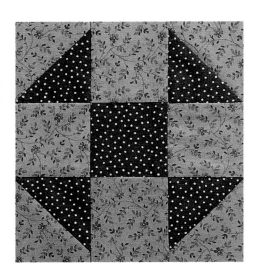

Nine Patch Block

A nine patch block consists of a square made up of nine smaller squares of equal size. These have colour variations that can create optical illusions or other interesting effects.

Begin by designing a block on graph paper. Each small square can be further divided into triangles to give more detail. Cut out templates from the graph paper (see page 122) and use them to mark patches onto your fabric. Cut out the patches (a). Join them by first piecing the small triangles to form squares (b). Press the seams to one side. Join the squares in rows (c), then join the rows to each other. Blocks can then be combined in various ways to make a larger project.

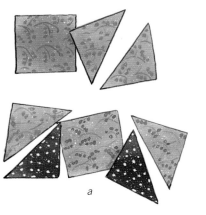

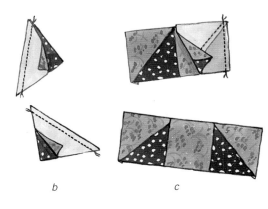

a

b

c

Variations on the Nine Patch Block

These variations are constructed in the same basic way as a nine patch block. However, the placing of the fabrics and the way in which the triangles and rectangles are combined gives a very different look.

To make a project more exciting, try joining blocks of different designs or rotate the blocks before joining them to create new overall patterns. Experiment on graph paper first or use a suitable computer programme.

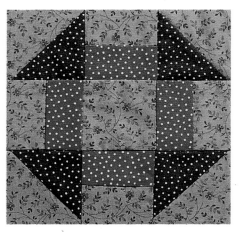

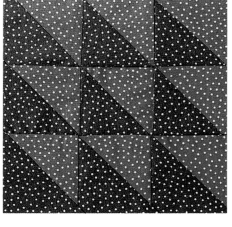

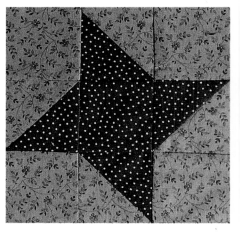

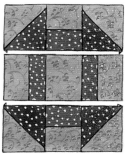

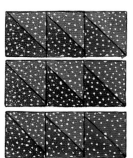

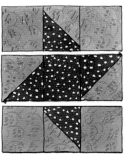

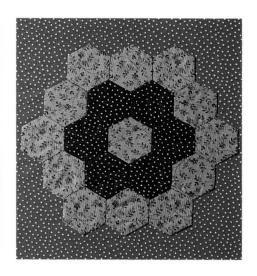

English Patchwork

English, or hexagonal, patchwork is a popular technique. The fabric patches are placed over paper shapes for accuracy, then pieced together by hand.

Two hexagonal templates are required for this technique. Craft shops supply these in a variety of sizes or you can make your own from stiff card. One template is used for marking out the paper shapes; the other template has a central 'window' for viewing the fabric before marking it. The window template is the larger of the two as it has a 6mm (¼in) seam allowance added.

Cut out the required number of paper shapes (old greetings cards are a good source of strong paper and the shapes can be re-used). Then cut out the fabric hexagons, using the window in the template to find a suitable area if your fabric has a printed design. Pin a paper template to the wrong side of a fabric hexagon and fold all the raw edges over to the back. Finger press them in place.

Take a needle and thread and stitch through the folded seam allowance and the paper from the back, leaving a 'tail' of thread hanging. Baste the seam allowance in place all round the patch, making creases at each corner to form a sharp point (a). Finish the thread by leaving another 'tail' before snipping. Repeat for all the hexagons.

Place two completed patches right sides together and, using matching thread, join them along one side with small overcasting stitches (b). Take care not to stitch into the paper. Continue to join patches together in this way, rethreading the needle when necessary. Once you have completed a project, press the patches before removing all the basting threads and paper shapes.

Template for paper shapes

Template for fabric patches, with 6mm (¼in) seam allowance added

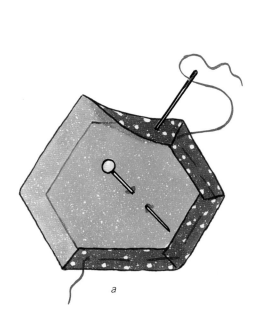

a

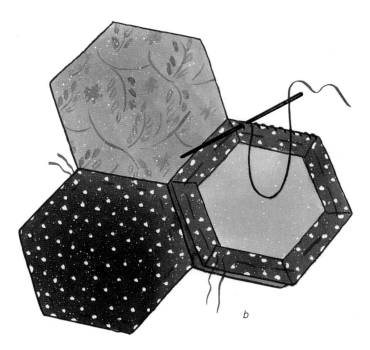

b

Cathedral Window Patchwork

Cathedral window patchwork is an ideal technique to do by hand. It looks fairly intricate, but if the fabric has been cut accurately in the first place, it should present no problems. Each cut square of fabric will finish just under half its original size.

The example shown was constructed from four 15 x 15cm (6 x 6in) squares. Always cut squares on the true grain of the fabric. Press the raw edges of each square under by 6mm (¼in) to hide the raw edges. Press two opposite corners diagonally together, then repeat the other way to show the centre of the square. Fold all four corners in to the centre and pin. Repeat by folding the new corners to the centre and pin (a). Using strong thread, secure the corners at the centre with a double cross stitch (b). The thread will show on the reverse.

To join two blocks, place them together and work overcasting stitches along one edge using a matching thread and picking up only a few fabric threads at a time (c). Finish off securely at the beginning and end of the seam.

Once you have joined at least four blocks, you can begin to add the patches for the 'windows'. Measure the square area as shown (d) to find the window size. Cut out an exact square of fabric for each window and pin it diagonally in place, covering the seam line. Roll back the edge of the 'frame' onto the raw edges of the window. The 'frame' will curve easily as it is on the bias. Neatly slipstitch the curved edges in place all around the window. Repeat for all the windows. By varying the colours of the windows, you can create all sorts of interesting designs.

a

b

c

d

Crazy Patchwork

This is a simple but effective technique that is perfect for recycling scraps of fabric. You can use any combination of fabrics you like, but choose colours that harmonize for the best result. Place the patches in a pleasing arrangement on a piece of foundation fabric. Overlap them if necessary but try to minimize bulk. Secure each patch to the foundation fabric with running stitch or a small machine zigzag stitch (a).

Once the foundation fabric has been covered with patches, these can be decorated with a variety of simple hand embroidery stitches (see below). Edge each patch with a decorative stitch, then add more detail by stitching motifs to the centre of a few of the larger patches (b).

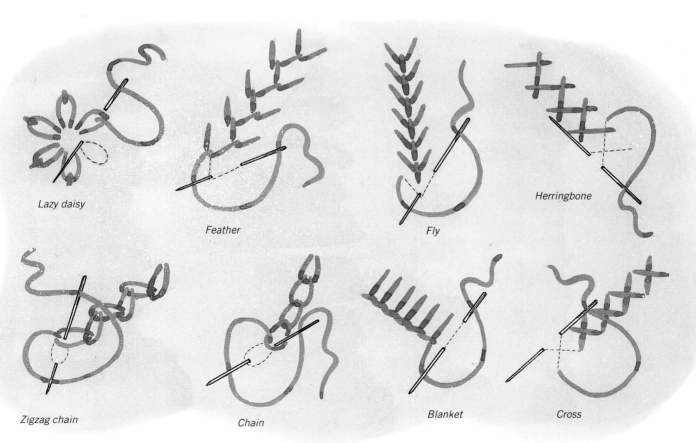

Lazy daisy

Feather

Fly

Herringbone

Zigzag chain

Chain

Blanket

Cross

Quilting Techniques

Quilting is a way of adding texture or warmth to a fabric that is either pieced or whole. Explore different types of wadding in sample form and use a variety of quilting techniques to build up an 'inspirations' folio before commencing larger projects.

Machine Quilting

It is simple to quilt using a sewing machine, especially with the variety of attachments currently available on the market. Many machines can now be set to produce a 'quilting' stitch that looks quite like hand quilting, and there are special machine feet (walking foot, dual feed lever or quilting foot) that help to feed your fabric through evenly and are useful for geometric designs. In the absence of these aids, an ordinary zigzag foot can be used instead. A size 14 (90) needle is the most suitable to cope with the thickness of the fabric in machine quilting.

You will normally need three layers for quilting – a backing fabric, wadding, and a top fabric. When quilting large projects, use quilters' safety pins to hold the layers in place (a). These are quick to remove and do not catch on the sewing foot in the way that basting stitches can. For smaller projects, baste the layers together with stitches arranged in a grid (b) or in lines that radiate out from the centre. Set the stitch length on the machine for about 12 stitches per 2.5cm (1in) and sew lines of quilting as you would a normal seam (c). Take care not to push the fabric through with your hands as this can cause the bottom layer to distort.

To quilt in random directions, such as when working vermicelli stitch (see page 135), change the presser foot to either a darning foot or an embroidery foot and lower the feed dog. Lower the presser foot bar and sew slowly with even stitches (d). To secure the thread at the end of a line of quilting, remove the fabric from the machine and turn to the reverse. Pull the thread end gently in order to bring the surface thread to the back. Knot both thread ends together and trim.

Alternatively, it is now acceptable to finish a line of quilting by sewing a few stitches 'on the spot' at the end of a line and simply clipping off the excess thread. The smaller the stitches, the less chance of the thread unravelling.

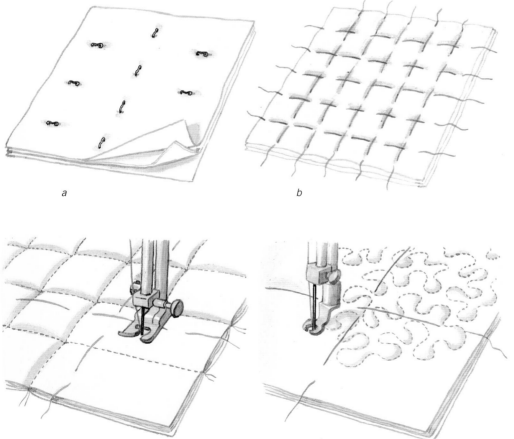

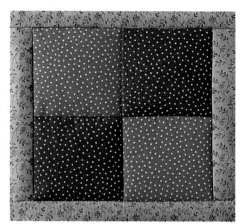

Stitching 'in the ditch'

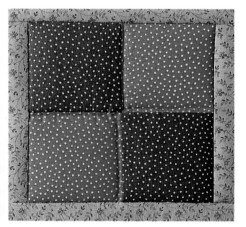

Stitching 6mm (¼in) away from seamline

Hand Quilting

As for machine quilting, you will be working with three layers – the backing fabric, the wadding and the top fabric. The thicker the wadding, the more quilted a project will look. There are specialist quilting threads available, but you could experiment with a variety of threads for a more unusual look. Use a short needle such as a 'between' or a special quilting needle (size 8).

Once you have transferred your design onto the fabric (see page 121) and basted the layers together (see opposite), you are ready to begin. It may be helpful to use a hoop or special quilting ring which is extra deep to take the thick layers. This will add a little tension to the 'sandwich', although it is best not to pull the fabric too taut as this will reduce the quilting effect. Try working both with and without a hoop to see which method suits you best.

Thread up your needle and make a knot at the end of the thread. Then pass the needle and thread down through the top layer and into the wadding. Bring the needle back out to the surface and

tug the thread so the knot pops into the wadding (a). Now quilt your design with small, even running stitches, taking care to go through all three layers (b). Practise to make sure that your stitches are even on the top and the reverse. Tug the thread gently as you go in order to create the soft quilted effect.

To finish off your thread securely, knot it around the end of the needle and push the knot down to the fabric. Take the needle down into the wadding layer only, then bring it up a short distance away and pull tightly until the knot pops into the wadding. Trim the surface thread and even out the fabric so that the loose end 'sinks' into the wadding.

The same stitching technique is used for quilting around block patchwork designs. You can position your quilting line 'in the ditch', i.e. along the seamline where two fabrics join (c). Alternatively, you can stitch 6mm (¼in) away from the seamline, preferably on the opposite side from the pressed seam allowance (d). Plan your quilting lines first before piecing and pressing.

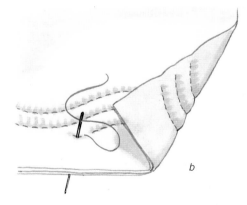

a

b

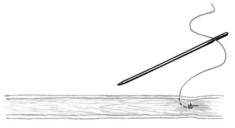

c

d

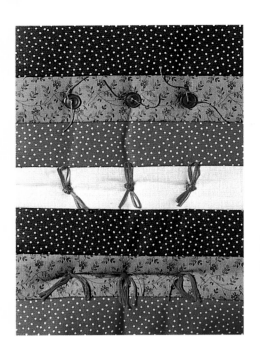

Knotted and Tied Quilting

When working on lightweight patchwork items that do not require a layer of wadding, it may not be appropriate to quilt them all over. However, it is still advisable to secure the top of the patchwork to the backing fabric by tying it at several points. Use a matching thread and oversew a few backstitches at appropriate points in the design (a).

Alternatively, on a padded project, you could make a feature of the knotting and tying as shown here. Secure the layers together with thick thread tied in bows (b) or sew on buttons (c) and ribbon bows at intervals to create a quilted look.

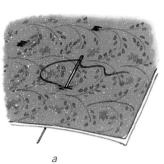

a

b

c

Trapunto Quilting

Trapunto quilting is a way of quilting specific areas of a project instead of all over. An extension of this is to work trapunto quilting on chosen sections first, then quilt the whole item again afterwards with a layer of wadding in the usual way. The areas of trapunto quilting will be raised above the rest.

To work trapunto quilting by hand, you will need a top fabric such as cotton and a soft backing fabric such as butter muslin. Baste the layers together. Make sure that the motif you wish to quilt is made of individual enclosed shapes. Stitch around each shape with small running stitches, leaving a tail of thread at the beginning and end which you can knot together to secure (a).

On the reverse (muslin) side, make a tiny slash along the centre of each motif (b). To fill the shapes, use quilting wool cut into small pieces or another soft stuffing. Push small pieces of the stuffing into the hole until the shape is filled. Do not overfill the shape as this will distort the fabric around it.

Close up the slash with oversewing stitches (c), pulling the thread tightly as you go to force the stuffing to the front. Repeat for all the motifs.

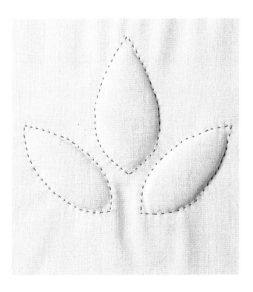

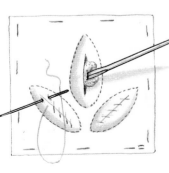

a

b

c

Shadow Trapunto Quilting

Shadow trapunto quilting is similar to trapunto quilting except that the top fabric is transparent, preferably organdie or organza (chiffon is too delicate). Quilt the motif as for trapunto quilting and slash the muslin on the reverse. However, instead of stuffing it with quilting wool, use tiny scraps of coloured fabric to fill the motif in order to create a diffused pattern. Sew up the slash with small stitches.

Shadow Quilting

You will need two layers of fabric for this attractive quilting technique: one for the backing and a transparent fabric for the top. The backing fabric can be coloured if you wish. You will also need some scraps of coloured fabric for the motifs.

Cut out the motifs and apply them to the right side of the backing fabric using adhesive fabric bond (a). Then lay the layer of transparent fabric over the top and baste it in place. Decorate over and around the motifs with either machine stitching (b) or hand stitches such as running stitch or backstitch (c) to secure the layers. When the quilting is complete, remove the basting stitches.

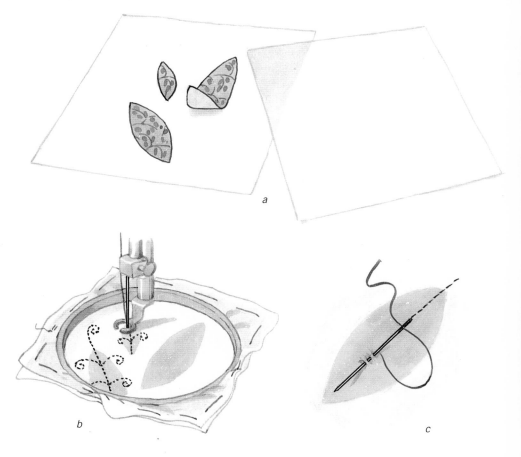

a

b

c

Free Machine Embroidery

Free machine embroidery allows you to stitch in any direction, smoothly building up textures and basically drawing with the machine. Patchwork and appliqué can be enhanced with machine embroidery and there is a huge variety of machine threads on the market, each with a specific use. It is a case of trial and error to find the threads that work best with your machine.

Setting Up

If you are working on a single layer of fabric, you will need an embroidery hoop in order to tension it for free machine embroidery: I prefer to use wooden hoops, as although slightly bulky they keep the fabric taut. The new spring-loaded plastic/metal hoops allow for easy repositioning of fabric but the tension is not as good.

The fabric must be tautly held in the embroidery hoop for successful free machine embroidery. It is often worth taking an additional step and binding the hoop's inner ring with a strip of cotton fabric to prevent the fabric from slipping.

Do be aware that not every machine will easily do free embroidery. Note that there are different types of presser foot, and modern machines usually have a number of different types. Your machine may not have a darning/embroidery foot attachment, but it is possible to stitch without a foot and use a bare needle – it just needs practice and great care. If you do not have a darning foot, do not bring your fingers anywhere near the unprotected needle when stitching. Keep them outside the embroidery hoop.

Preparing the Machine

There are some basic steps to take in order to set up your machine for the techniques which follow. Once you have set it as instructed below, try the two techniques described on the opposite page.

1 Lower the feed dog (zigzag teeth) if possible or cover with a darning plate if you have one. If not, clear sticky tape stuck down over the feed will also do.
2 Set the stitch width dial to zero.
3 Set the stitch length dial to zero.
4 Check the tension in the bobbin and top thread according to the manufacturer's recommendation. The top tension should be set in the middle of the dial and the bobbin

thread should come away when tugged. It should not run freely.
5 If your machine has programmed stitches, set it for straight stitch.

Using Free Machining for Colouring

It is possible to add texture and solid areas of colour with free machine embroidery – and it is a much quicker method than using appliqué techniques.

Practise building up solid shapes or areas of colour simply by stitching back and forth over your fabric, using the needle as if it is a coloured pencil. A common mistake is to overstitch on the one spot and if this happens the fabric may distort badly or the thread may break, both of which can be very frustrating to the novice machine embroiderer, but you will soon learn to avoid this.

Other Techniques with Free Machining

Once you have built up a little skill, it is also possible to free machine using a zigzag stitch to build up small solid blocks and wavy lines of colour. And by turning the stitch width dial as you sew, lines of varying width can be created. Always sew slowly and carefully when using this technique.

TIPS

If you find problems occurring once you start stitching, check the following points:
- the presser foot has been lowered
- the needle is sharp – change for a new one if necessary
- tension in the top and bobbin
- the fabric is tight enough in the hoop
- some metallic threads work better if the top tension has been slackened off a bit

Doodling

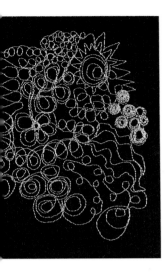

Frame the fabric in an embroidery hoop and lay the flat of the fabric against the bed of the machine. Turn the needle control to pick up the bobbin thread, bringing it through to the surface. Then re-insert the needle into the fabric and lower the presser foot lever even if you are using no presser foot. Now begin to stitch by slowly pressing the foot pedal and moving the hoop, keeping your hands either side of the hoop. Press the pedal harder but keep the hoop moving – move it slowly to keep the stitches small. By moving the hoop faster, large jagged stitch effects can be created. Stitch back and forth in order to build up areas of colour or stitch freely in any direction, overlapping the threads. Trim excess threads off close to the fabric surface. The smaller the stitch, the less likely the cut thread will unravel.

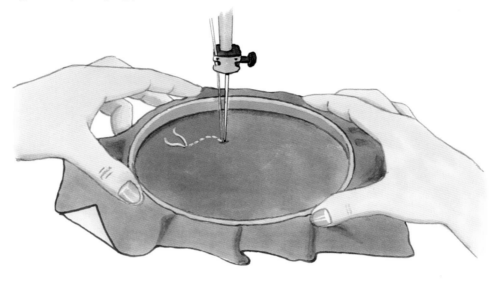

Vermicelli

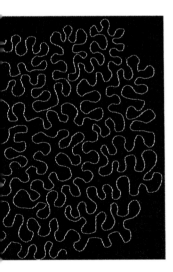

Vermicelli is Italian for 'small worms' and this stitch allows for a pattern to be built up by stitching in and out to create small wavy lines. Place the fabric in an embroidery hoop to ensure correct tension and thread up the machine for free machine embroidery. Lay the flat of the fabric against the bed of the machine. Stitch back and forth continuously in waves, taking care not to overlap any lines. Ensure all the background fabric is covered with stitched lines. To make the surface more interesting use a variegated colour thread.

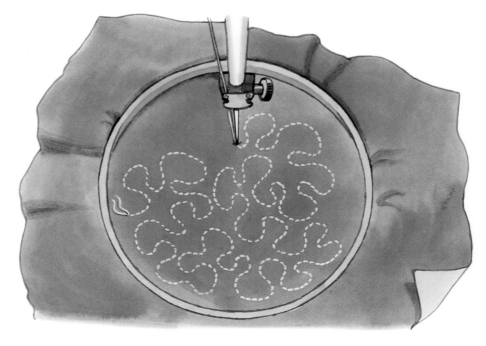

Machine Appliqué

Machine appliqué is a development of machine embroidery and the speed at which you can achieve stunning results is very satisfying. Keep the stitches neat and close together so you can trim the thread ends back to the surface without fear of them unravelling.

Fabric Bond Appliqué

Layers of colour can be built up and overlapped using this technique. It also prevents fabric from fraying and slipping and so is ideal for fabrics which are otherwise difficult to apply. Begin by ironing a layer of fabric bond onto the reverse of the fabric to be applied (a). Cut out the desired shape, peel off the paper backing from the bond (b) and place the motif glue-side down onto the background fabric. Iron in place (c). Now decorate with machine embroidery (d). Try a few types of fabric bond to find out which kind suits your project best as sometimes the bond is very stiff and prevents the finished fabric from draping.

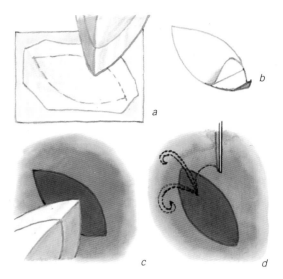

Satin Stitch Appliqué

Trim, pin and baste the chosen motif to the background fabric (a). Set the machine to normal and use the zigzag foot. Raise the feed dog if lowered, and set the stitch width to its widest setting and the stitch length to 0.5. Slowly satin stitch around the edge of the motif (b). Turn corners by keeping the needle in the fabric, raising the presser foot, turning the fabric, lowering the presser foot and then continuing to stitch. You may need to vary the stitch width and length in order to achieve a smooth satin stitch. It may also help to lower the top tension by one in order for the thread to run through freely.

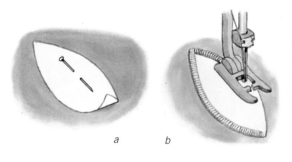

Three-dimensional Appliqué

This works well for natural motifs such as flowers, insects, and fish scales. Plan your motif as you would for ordinary machine appliqué but pinch it in a little by gathering or pleating by hand before stitching it down at one point only (e.g. the top of the fuchsia cone as illustrated in figs a–c). You can press folds with an iron or baste to secure if preferred. Add extra detail with free machine embroidery before or after applying the motif.

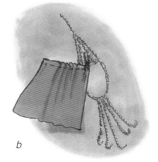

Dyeing and Colouring Fabrics

Commercial fabric colours are sometimes a little too flat and a patchwork project can look truly original if it is based on hand-dyed fabrics. There are many methods for dyeing fabrics and it takes time to find the method that you like or that will work for a particular project. I like to use Procion dyes but the quantity of dye powder required will vary from manufacturer to manufacturer. The following cold water method works best on natural fabrics.

Materials and Equipment

- 50cm (20in) square of cotton fabric
- Procion dye powder (assorted colours)
- Jam jars
- Plastic tubs and bucket
- Measuring jug
- Household salt
- Washing soda crystals
- Rubber gloves
- Metal tablespoon
- Metal teaspoon

Method

1 Soak your chosen fabric in hot water in order to remove any starch and to allow the dye take up to be consistent.

2 Mix up the salt and soda solutions in the quantities given below. **Remember** that the soda solution will be further diluted before use.

Salt solution: 55g (2oz) salt to 560ml (20fl oz) hot water
Soda solution: 110g (4oz) soda to 420ml (15fl oz) hot water

3 Use a jam jar and wear rubber gloves to mix the dye powder with hot water – try a teaspoon of dye powder to half a jar of hot water and add a tablespoon of salt solution. Stir well.

4 Place your damp fabric in a plastic bucket and pour over the dye mix. Depending on the effect you want, keep moving the fabric to allow the dye take-up to be even or scrunch or knot the fabric before placing in the dye bath for a more random effect. You can also use a spoon to splatter a different colour of dye over a different area of the fabric. The dye colours will eventually soak through and bleed into each other, creating new colour combinations.

5 Leave the fabric in the dye for at least 10 minutes, then carefully pour off the excess dye (this can be used for another fabric).

6 Mix three tablespoons of the soda solution with 850ml (30fl oz) of cold water and pour this into the bucket until the fabric is just covered.

7 Leave to fix for 30 minutes, then rinse the fabric under a cold tap until the water runs clear. There may always be a slight discharge of colour from home-dyed fabrics.

8 Leave the fabric to dry either by hanging it outside or using a tumble dryer. Avoid drying over a radiator as the heat is dispersed unevenly and you may get dark lines on your fabric. It also stiffens the fabric.

Joining Blocks

An easy way of making a large quilt without working with a cumbersome amount of fabric and wadding is to quilt small sections, or blocks, and then join each block together to form the overall design. You can add a decorative sashing for extra effect.

Joining Blocks with Sashing

For this method, the backing fabric, wadding and top fabric should be the same size. Quilt the blocks by hand or machine, leaving 6mm (¼in) around each block unquilted. Cut two strips (sashing) in a contrasting or matching colour to join the blocks. The strips should be the length of the block by the desired width (this will vary depending on the overall size of your project) plus a 6mm (¼in) seam allowance on each long edge. Cut a strip of wadding slightly narrower than one of the sashing strips in order to leave the seam allowance free. Pin and baste in place. Pin the padded sashing strip to the decorative side of the first block and the other strip to the back, right sides together and raw edges matching (a). Stitch through all layers, taking a 6mm (¼in) seam allowance.

Open out the padded sashing strip and join it to the second block, right sides together, taking a 6mm (¼in) seam allowance (b). Fold over the unpadded sashing strip to cover the join, turn under the raw edge by 6mm (¼in) and pin to the reverse of the second block. Slip stitch in place (c). Join the blocks to make rows, then join the rows together using the same method.

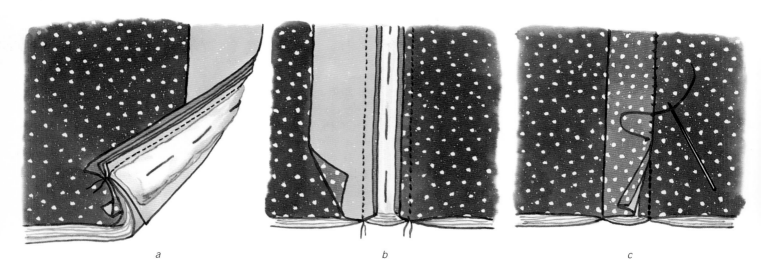

a

b

c

Joining Blocks without Sashing

Plan your design first, as you will need to add a 6mm (¼in) seam allowance around each block. Cut the backing fabric for each block 2.5cm (1in) larger all around than the wadding and top. (For clarity in the diagrams below, only one edge of the backing fabric is shown larger.) Quilt the block by hand or machine, following your chosen design, leaving about 1.3cm (½in) unquilted all around the top fabric for ease of joining.

To join two blocks, place them right sides together and pin just the top layers together, taking a 6mm (¼in) seam allowance. Do not catch in the wadding or backing fabric.

Stitch the top layers together (a). Open out the blocks and finger press the seam to one side. Make sure the wadding edges just touch; trim away any excess if necessary (b). Stitch the wadding together with large cross stitches in a matching thread (c).

Lay the edge of one piece of backing fabric over the join. Trim the other piece back by 2cm (¾in) and finger press a 6mm (¼in) seam allowance under. Lay the folded edge on top of the other piece of backing fabric and slipstitch in place, using an appropriate thread colour (d). Join the blocks together in rows, then join the rows in the same way.

a

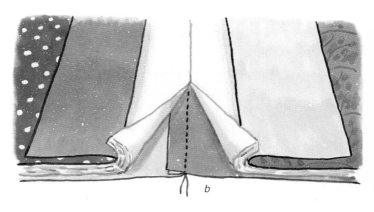

b

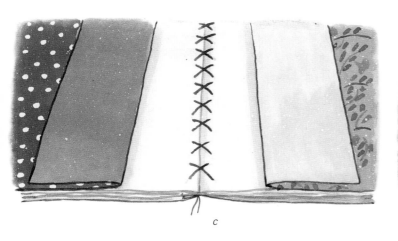

c

d

Finishing Quilt Edges

There are many ways to finish quilt projects. It depends on the size of the finished piece and its final use. It may be appropriate simply to fold finish a large bed throw where the edges are not going to be a feature, whereas a baby quilt or a fashion item might benefit from a decorative edge such as Somerset points or a gathered frill.

Fold Finish

Trim back just the wadding by 1.5cm (⅝in), leaving the top fabric and the backing fabric free. Press all the raw edges under by 1cm (⅜in). When you reach a corner, overlap the raw edges at right angles for a neat finish. Slipstitch the folded edges together all around the quilt.

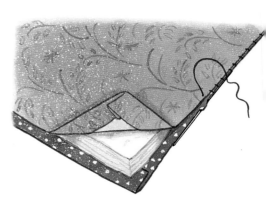

Backing as Binding

Leave the backing fabric slightly larger all round than the wadding and top fabric – by about 2.5cm (1in). Press the raw edges of the backing fabric under by 5mm (³⁄₁₆in) (a) and fold up the remaining fabric to the top of the quilt. Pin in place, then slipstitch.

To create simple mitred corners, keep one edge of the binding straight and overlap the other edge where they meet, tucking under the excess binding at a 45° angle first. Pin and slipstitch in place (b).

a   b   c

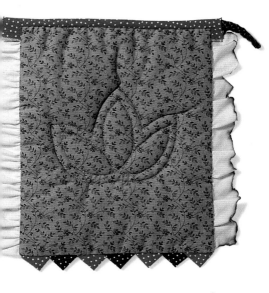

Piped Edging

For this edging (see left, top edge), cut parallel strips of fabric on the bias wide enough to cover your piping cord plus 2cm (¾in) extra for the seam allowance. Join strips to make up the required length (a). Turn the short raw edges under for a neat finish. Wrap the fabric lengthways around the piping cord. Pin, then stitch along close to the cord, using a zipper foot (b).

Pin the piping around the edge of your quilt with raw edges matching. Butt the two ends together where they meet (c). Baste in place. Lay the backing fabric on top, right sides together, and sew all around, taking a 1cm (⅜in) seam allowance. Leave a gap in one edge long enough to turn the quilt right side out. Turn out and press, then slipstitch the gap closed.

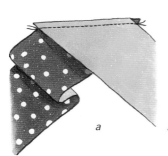

a

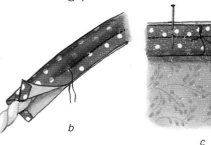

b

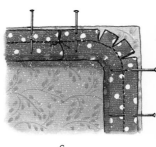

c

Burnt Edge Frill

This edging (see above, right edge) works best on experimental projects. Cut a strip of silk 2cm (¾in) wider than the desired finished width by twice the finished length + 1cm (⅜in). Use a lit birthday cake candle to burn along one edge of the silk strip, creating a wavy line. For safety, work over a sink with a running tap. Gather the frill and attach to the quilt as for Piped Edging above.

Frilled Edging

Cut a strip of fabric twice the width of the finished frill + 2cm (¾in) by twice the finished length + 1cm (⅜in). Fold the strip in half lengthways, wrong sides together, and press. Fold under the short raw edges at each end by 5mm (³⁄₁₆in) and press. Thread up a needle,

knot the thread end, then work running stitch along the length of the frill, joining the raw edges together (a). Pull up the thread to gather the frill to the required length, then knot the thread end (b). Attach the frill to the quilt (see above, left edge) as for the Piped Edging above.

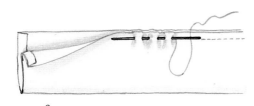

a

b

Prairie Points

These triangles (see above, lower edge) make an unusual edging. Cut a square of fabric 6 x 6cm (2⅜ x 2⅜in) (a). Fold in half diagonally to make a triangle and finger press (b). Fold in half to make a smaller triangle. All the cut edges should now be along the long edge (c). Place the triangles in a row on the right side of the fabric, overlapping them if desired. Attach as for the previous edges shown, but only take a 5mm (³⁄₁₆in) seam allowance in order to leave the bulk of the points showing (d).

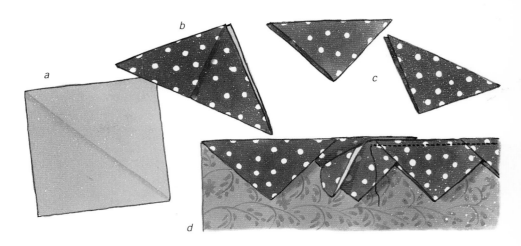

a

b

c

d

Glossary

Appliqué A method of applying one fabric onto a background fabric in a decorative manner

Baste Work large running stitches to mark guidelines onto fabric or to stitch two fabrics together temporarily

Bias The diagonal line across a piece of fabric which has the most stretch or 'give'

Bias binding Strips of fabric cut on the bias that can be joined together and used to edge projects. The raw edges of bias strips are pressed under first. Bias strips curve easily around corners due to the stretch in the fabric

Binding Strips of fabric cut on the straight grain of the fabric that can be used to edge projects. Ideal for quilts where the corners are squared off

Blocks A specially designed geometric method of piecing together fabric in a particular pattern, e.g. nine patch block, Flying Geese block. Blocks can be joined together to make larger projects

Bonding powder A fabric glue available in fine grains rather like salt. It is scattered over one fabric before laying another fabric on top and fusing together with a hot iron

Chain sewing A method of sewing patches together in one continuous chain or line. There is no need to trim the threads between each set of patches as long as the patches are placed into the machine close together. Threads can be snipped afterwards

Darning/embroidery foot A special attachment that allows for multi-directional sewing (known as free machine embroidery)

Dual feed foot/lever Machines are now available with this foot or function that ensures both the top and bottom layers of fabric are fed through at exactly the same speed, eliminating puckers or gathers in the fabric

Fat quarters A cut quarter of a metre length of fabric, i.e. 50cm x half the fabric width. The term 'fat' refers to the fact that the quarter is usually wider than it is long

Feed dog The zigzag teeth on the bed of a sewing machine that help feed the fabric through

Free machine embroidery A method of machine embroidery using a hoop and a darning foot that allows the embroiderer to stitch in any direction. It can also be worked without a machine foot

Fringing The cut, frayed edge left when the horizontal threads are withdrawn from a fabric. Fringing can be done using the point of a pin or a teazel

Fusible fabric bond An iron-on glue webbing useful for sticking two layers of fabric together (e.g. for appliqué techniques)

Mitred corner A binding cut or folded into a 45° angle in order to give a crisp finish to a corner

Omnigrid A transparent plastic ruler used for measuring patchwork templates

Presser foot The foot on a sewing machine that guides the fabric through

Presser foot lever The bar on a sewing machine that is pressed to activate the top tension and lower the presser foot

Quilt foot/walking foot A sewing machine attachment specially designed to feed thick layers of fabric through evenly

Quilter's quarter A clear plastic rule which adds 6mm (¼in) accurately to straight edges when marking a seam allowance around patches

Rouleau strip A narrow strip of fabric cut on the bias, sewn to make a tube and turned the right way out using a special rouleau turner or fine hook

Selvedges The finished edges of a woven piece of fabric. They run up both the right and left sides and usually look like tightly woven bands of the same cloth

Stitch in the ditch A method of quilting in between patches by working exactly along the seam line in order to hide the quilting stitches

Tack See **Baste**

Teazel A natural dried bristle brush or man-made metal brush used for fluffing up fabric or fraying edges

Templates These are either trace-off patterns for appliqué designs, or card shapes which can be traced around to mark patches onto fabric before cutting out

Skein A length of wool or thread as sold

Water soluble fabric A fabric that dissolves in water after embroidery to reveal a lacy stitched motif. It is available in either hot or cold water formats

Water/air soluble pens Fabric markers for drawing template lines. Can be washed out or left to vanish

Index

ACKNOWLEDGEMENTS
The author would like to thank the following people for their help and encouragement during the writing of the book:
  My husband Morph and son for being so understanding during the chaos.
  My parents, with love, for their support and babysitting services.
  My mum-in-law for typing up my scribbles with ease and cheerfulness.
  Also all the stitchers for interpreting my rather free sketches so well.
  Thanks to Sally and Julie at Coats for the threads and canvas, as well as to Mr and Mrs Deutsch, Jane and the staff at Mandors for all the sumptuous fabrics.
  Finally, a massive thank you to Patsy North for patience and help throughout this book.

Designers:
Crazy patchwork quilt, Beaded hat band, Slashed patchwork throw:
Liz McLean McKay, Toronto, Canada
Autumn leaf quilt: Ann Paterson, Dunoon, Scotland

Stitchers:
Cora Ham, Toni Hanley, Morren Roche, Pauline Simpson, Sheena Walker

Suppliers:
Coats Crafts UK
The Lingfield Estate
McMullen Road
Darlington
DL1 1YQ

Mandors Textile Centre
1 Scott Street
Glasgow
G3 6NU